new classic cocktails

new classic cocktails

GARY REGAN

and

MARDEE HAIDIN REGAN

Wiley Publishing, Inc.

Photography copyright © 1997 by
Lisa Koenig

Published by Wiley Publishing, Inc.,
New York, NY

Library of Congress Cataloging-in-Publication Data
Regan, Gary
   New classic cocktails/Gary Regan and
   M. Haidin Regan
         p.   cm.
   Includes biographical references and index.
   ISBN 0-7645-6706-3
   Cocktails. I. Regan, M. Haidin. II. Title.
   TX951.R365   96-40035
   641.8'74—dc21   CIP

Cover photographs by Lisa Koenig

Cover Design by Jeff Faust

Book Design by Nick Anderson

Manufactured in the United States of America

10 9 8 7 6 5 4 3 2 1

CONTENTS

Bibliography/
Mail–Order Sources 131

Index 132

ACKNOWLEDGMENTS

The main players who helped with this book are detailed on the pages that follow, but we should take this opportunity to thank each and every bartender and chef who donated recipes, spent time phoning, faxing, and carefully explaining exactly how each drink was made. These are the men and women who hold the future of the cocktail in their hands. Thanks should also go to the people who submitted recipes that aren't included here—the drinks were all delightful.

Thanks also to Ray Foley, publisher of *Bartender* magazine, who is always there when we need him; Ted Haigh, a.k.a. Dr. Cocktail, who keeps us entertained on the World Wide Web; Mike Veach and Chris Morris, of United Distillers (Louisville), who are constant sources of incredible information; Bill Samuels, Jr., president of Maker's Mark; Nicola Blazier of the Four Seasons Hotel chain; Leslie Lefkowitz of the Ritz-Carlton (New York City); Andrew Freeman and Robin Massey of Rainbow (New York City); Nicole Resman of Mesa Grill/Bolo (New York City); Richard O. Barbour of Toucano America (Darien, Connecticut); Margie Blaum, delightful assistant to Chef Paul Prudhomme; Kenneth Jaworski of Mercury (Miami Beach); Sam Iodannis of the Four Seasons Resort (Nevis,

British West Indies); Jeff Pogash and Patrick Morley Fletcher of Schieffelin and Somerset Co. (New York City); Joanna Stein of the Lark Creek Inn (Larkspur, California); Samara Farber of David Kratz & Co. (New York City); Michael Howett of Marion's (New York City); Pat Schloeman of Frontera Grill/Topolobampo (Chicago); Scott Sternbach of Grange Hall (New York City); Adam Seger of the Seelbach Hotel (Louisville); Patrick Colombo of Sfuzzi (Dallas); Joni Friedman of Tait Farm Foods (Centre Hall, Pennsylvania); Rhonda Findley of Concepts by Staib (Little Rock); Mary Donna Moceri of Vallone Restaurant Group (Houston); Harry Denton of Harry Denton's Starlight Room (San Francisco); Bill Kimpton of the Kimpton Group (San Francisco); Karl Bruno of the Alexis Hotel (Seattle); Penny Glazier of Monkey Bar and Tapika (New York City); Maria Pico and Fernando Hernandez of Rums of Puerto Rico (New York City); Sari Seiken of Hill and Knowlton (New York City); Larry Wolhandler, Salvatore Buttiglieri, and Donna Hammond of Painter's Tavern (Cornwall-on-Hudson, New York).

For graciously lending their homes, gardens, pools, restaurants, and nearly all their worldly goods for location photographs in Cornwall-on-Hudson, we would like to thank our friends and neighbors the intrepid Stephan Wilkinson, Susan Crandell, and Brook Wilkinson; Annie Armstrong, eye extraordinaire; Michael and the very real Ellen Kelly; and Jerome and Gloria Brisman.

For patience, wit, professionalism, a keen eye, and long legs, we would like to thank photographer Lisa Koenig and her more-than-able assistant, Rainer "Beefcake" Fehringer.

Thanks also to the artists who supplied works of art for use as backdrops in some of the photographs: *Bartender* by Robert Lederman, in the background of Nikos at Nite, page 84; *The Lemon* by Jimi Ferrara, in the background of the Hennessy Martini, on page 54; and *This Is What It Comes To*, by Stephen Rosen and Larry Wolhandler, in the background of Painter's Punch, on page 90.

As always, thanks to our incredibly talented agent, Michael Carlisle, at the William Morris Agency, and his helpful assistants, Arnold Kim and Mary Beth Brown.

Many, many thanks to Justin Schwartz, our editor at Macmillan Publishing, who first recognized that this topic was worthy of a book and whose patience is unmatched in the world of publishing. Amy Gordon has been a blessing, and we greatly appreciate all her help.

And finally, thanks to all our friends who have gone without their favorite drinks when we insisted they try these new ones. Some have been converted.

INTRODUCTION

"Why is it," asked a fellow cocktail fancier in the not too distant past, "that over-consumption of beverage alcohol is politically incorrect, and yet the Monkey Bar  is packed five deep every evening and each and every customer is balancing an enormous cocktail glass?"

Food for thought. Our immediate reaction was to explain that although it's not seemly to get snockered by tippling shots of cheap whiskey in some five-and-dime joint where the bartender's apron gets washed every third week, it has once again become socially acceptable to sip monumental Martinis. Just be sure that the cocktail glasses have the thinnest of stems, the maître d' wears an Armani tuxedo, and you aren't going to be driving home.

Indeed, cocktails are back. And it's not just the Three Ms—Martini, Manhattan, and Margarita—drinkers are ordering enough Stingers and Old-Fashioneds and Pimm's Cups that you'd think it was the Fifties and early Sixties all over again. Classic cocktails are here to stay. Furthermore, modern master bartenders are infatuated with the increasing variety of new liquors on the market and are creating their own drinks: the Cosmopolitan, the Metropolitan, and the International, among them. Many of these modern masterpieces share the qualities of the classics: They are simple in design yet complex in character and flavor. They are what we call *new classic cocktails*.

It has been a long, somewhat boring, two decades since American barrooms have seen glasses full of mysterious potions of myriad hues. But the craft of creating cocktails—or mixology, if you must—never really died, it merely slumbered for a while after a few too many badly built Singapore Slings. What events led to the resurgence of the cocktail? To find an answer, we must look to our recent past.

In the mid-1970s, when we first heard the beat of the electronic drums that tried in vain to warn us of white suits and disco music, swinging singles were ordering doubles of whatever took their fancy: Dirty Rivers flowed down the bar, Slings were slung, and dedicated quaffers mused on Golden Dreams while Grasshoppers and Pink Squirrels hammered Rusty Nails into Sidecars and Brave Bulls trampled Scorpions for one sip of an ice-cold Daiquiri. In the Seventies, psychedelia didn't always come on blotter paper.

Seemingly, however, the end of that decade (and the demise of disco) heralded a hiatus for cocktails. The early Eighties was a dismal time for bartenders. Jane and Joe Public had a change of heart, and although a few die-hards continued to demand Martinis dry and Manhattans sweet, most folk seemed content to sip on glasses of what they called Chablis; the occasional gin and tonic; blended scotch on the rocks; and that most boring of drinks, the White Wine Spritzer. The fizz was gone from the fizz water, Brandy Alexander was better known as a porn star, and the Godfather lay dead in the garden. It was time to regroup, reflect on our wild and crazy past, and figure out the meaning of moderation.

Celebrities were showing us the way. It seemed, for a while, as though there couldn't possibly be an empty bed at the Betty Ford Clinic; and many people who made it out of the Seventies alive, but in need of a little help to face their new sobriety, took shelter in twelve-step programs. For the most part, the respite from overconsumption was welcome. America had spent a long night under the table; dawn was upon us, and we were undergoing a metamorphosis of sorts. Nobody, however, expected to be jolted out of the slumber by the crashing and cranking of the next wave of cocktail phenomena.

Sex on the Beach is the first mixed drink we can remember that was ordered more because people enjoyed speaking its name out loud than because it tasted so darned good. But Sex on the Beach was somewhat tame in name compared to the drinks that took center stage a few years later. In the mid-1980s, punk cocktails staggered up to the bar to be counted. What's a punk cocktail? The term is one that we use to describe drinks such as the Brain Hemorrhage (Baileys Irish Cream with Chambord dashed on top). It resembles a brain from a 1950s sci-fi movie, complete with crimson veins. The Brain Hemorrhage isn't a classic drink by any stretch of the imagination, but people loved to order it. And perhaps most important, the Brain Hemorrhage and its followers—the Abortion, Windex, the Lonely Lesbian, Anti-Freeze, and others with names even more offensive—often looked as disgusting as they sounded.

Punk cocktails, like punk music, let anyone get into the act. Even those who didn't have a clue to how to make a proper Martini could still throw a lot of different liquors and fruit juices into a glass and wait to see what happened. However, we must also consider the monkeys-at-the-typewriters theory here: Whoever thought, for instance, that mixing together rum, gin, vodka, tequila, triple sec, lemon juice, and cola would produce a decent drink? Although it might not deserve a place among the classics, the Long Island Iced Tea works well despite its unorthodox combination of components. Thus popular new drinks are sometimes born from good luck rather than an intimate knowledge of the cocktail shaker.

Other drinks followed suit: The Screaming Nazi, Surfers on Acid, and Roadkill made their way into our glasses; and Liquid Heroin, Liquid Cocaine, and the Russian Quaalude were legally consumed in bars across the nation. Perhaps the most disgusting drink of the era was Cottage Cheese: Take a shot of Baileys Irish Cream, hold it in your mouth, and follow it with a shot of Rose's Lime Juice; the lime juice curdles the Irish Cream and the drink feels like a mouthful of cottage cheese. Ugh. And one more drink phenomenon should be recorded here, if only to demonstrate just how desperate the bartenders of the mid-1980s were: A bar that was known as King Tut's Wah Wah Hut, deep in the heart of New York City's East Village, posted a sign outside its doors that advertised a drink made with NyQuil as the base "liquor." It was probably a nightcap.

Jell-O shots were another curiosity of the Eighties that are still in vogue with younger drinkers today. Take a package of Jell-O, add hot water and cold vodka (or any other liquor), chill well, and feel it slide down your throat. Yes, it's a sophomoric concept. According to the lovable late Richard Sax in his book *Classic Home Desserts*, the drink has actually been around since the Fifties; but its resurgence in the Eighties is yet another example of just how reckless the cocktail drinkers of that decadent decade were. We needed new drinks; and without punk cocktails as an impetus, we might never have seen some of the new classics highlighted in these pages. Punk cocktails smartly slapped the classicist bartenders across the face and screamed, "*Create*, goddamn it, *create*." And some took note.

But while all this was happening, another sensation occurred that would also help point the way toward new classic cocktails: The drinking classes turned again to straight liquor. Instead of the indiscriminate swigging of whatever was cheap and turned them on that defined the sippers of the Seventies, this time, only the best of the best would suffice. Single-malt scotches came into vogue; and a few short years later, all varieties of top-shelf liquors were being sipped at bars across the country. Small-batch bourbons, XO cognacs, and 100-percent agave tequilas were being poured into oversized snifters and savored by a new breed of spirits connoisseurs. And, strangely enough, all this sophisticated sipping was most probably a result of lobbying by temperance advocates.

In the mid-nineteenth century, when the temperance movement was first gaining momentum, its advocates promoted moderation, not abstinence. But by the first decades of the twentieth century, when the Anti-Saloon League successfully lobbied for the complete abolition of bars and beverage alcohol, moderation was no longer an option. Luckily, the temperance groups that sprang up almost a century later returned to the original purpose of their forebears: They sought only moderation. These groups had a legitimate cause. Many of their members' lives had been damaged or ruined as a direct result of alcohol abuse. But their mission was to stop people from driving with too much alcohol in their bloodstream and to stop them from drinking completely only if their habit caused harm to themselves or others. An admirable cause, and one to which the beverage industry reacted commendably.

For the most part, the beer, wine, and liquor companies applauded the efforts of groups such as Mothers Against Drunk Driving (MADD) and started to appeal to consumers to drink in moderation. The result? Drinkers still wanted their dram, and they still had a certain amount of money in their pockets; but instead of spending that cash on copious quantities of low-grade fuel, they ordered small portions of the best liquors, hand-crafted ales and lagers, and fine wines when they were out on the town. And they invested in a bevy of specialty bottlings for at-home entertaining. Faith Popcorn's predic-

tion of cocooning came true; but, oh, what delights were purchased to fill these designer cocoons. "Quality rather than quantity" became the most overused phrase in every liquor-related magazine and newspaper article.

Infused liquors also played a part in the cocktail revolution. The practice of adding fruits, herbs, and vegetables to distilled spirits probably dates to the Middle Ages, when alchemists sought to preserve the properties of various herbs so that soldiers could carry them onto the battlefield for medicinal relief. Famed New Orleans chef Paul Prudhomme was probably the first to popularize infusions when he introduced his Cajun Martini back in 1980, but it was Finlandia vodka that took the ball and ran with it some ten years later. Now, it's hard to find a decent bar that doesn't display a decanter filled with fruits and vodka, peppers and tequila, or bourbon and peaches.

The stage was set: Modern sophisticates were sipping top-shelf spirits, the younger crowd was shooting newly created cocktails with strange-sounding names, and the advent of infused spirits—both homemade and produced by distillers—provided us with more flavors of liquor than ever before. Enter the classicist bartenders, the men and women who took the best ingredients and mixed them well, creating the new classic drinks of the 1990s.

The Evolution of the Cocktail

No one knows who invented the cocktail. We're not even sure precisely when the word first was used to describe a spirituous drink. Taken literally, it seems that we are discussing the tail of a male chicken, but why would that apply? Stories and theories abound: Some are tall tales; some are short anecdotes; one or two are strangely feasible; but most are, at the very least, entertaining.

There's an oft-told tale of Betsy Flanagan, a pro-Revolutionary innkeeper, who is said to have stolen chickens from pro-British neighbors to feed Washington's troops. The story holds that she garnished the patriots' drinks with the roosters' tail feathers—a rather Madame Defarge–like gesture to be sure—and offered the toast, "Vive le cock tail!"

Another theory claims that the cocktail was so-named because its various hues were reminiscent of the many colors of a rooster's tail. The first American edition of *Larousse Gastronomique* (1961) includes this interesting but confusing possible derivation, among others, ". . . according to certain etymologists, because the primitive cocktail of the Manhattan pioneers consisted in cocks' tails, dipped in a concoction of pimentos with which they tickled their throats to incite them to drink."

One somewhat believable story is detailed in *Famous New Orleans Drinks & how to mix 'em*, by

Stanley Clisby Arthur, and this one concerns apothecary Antoine Amedée Peychaud, a late-eighteenth-century refugee from San Domingo who settled in the Big Easy and opened a shop on Royal Street. Peychaud is best known for his eponymous bitters, but Arthur claims that he dispensed drinks made from brandy and bitters to customers who needed a stomach remedy, and he served these drinks in egg cups. Peychaud's native language was French, and so he would have referred to an egg cup as a *coquetier* (KO-keh-tee-ay); and Arthur contends that it was the Anglicization of this word that resulted in *cocktail*. The story of Peychaud and his bitters is well documented, and the timing of the story is perfect; so this tale could, indeed, be true.

In *The Dictionary of Drink and Drinking* (1965), Oscar A. Mendelsohn suggests a few theories for the origin of the word *cocktail*: One story tells of a Mexican Indian maiden named Xochtil who served a mixed drink to an American soldier (Mendelsohn notes that this is "among the crazier theories"), and another suggests that the drink is intended to "cock the tail," meaning, more or less, to put one in high spirits. In *Straight Up or On the Rocks* (1993), William Grimes suggests that the word may have been derived from a drink known as Cock Ale, which, according to Mendelsohn, came from a seventeenth-century recipe book called *Compleat Housewife*. And according to *The Dictionary of American Food and Drink* (1983), by John F. Mariani, this same theory was also put forth by none other than H. L. Mencken in 1945.

Our favorite tale of the origin of the word was documented by George Bishop in his delightful book *The Booze Reader: A Soggy Saga of Man In His Cups* (1965). Bishop contends that the word stems from the English *cock-tail*, which "referred to a woman of easy virtue who was considered desirable but impure." Desirable but impure: Is there a better way to describe a cocktail? Impure, not only because it is a combination of different ingredients but also because the first sip of a cocktail makes us all feel, well, just a little daring. When we take a cocktail to our lips we are embarking on an exciting adventure, and the results can be positively scandalous, but oh so very desirable.

But what defines a cocktail? The first bartender to gain fame and fortune as a master of his craft was Professor Jerry Thomas, a mid-nineteenth-century bartender and entrepreneur who is described in the preface to his 1862 book, *How to Mix Drinks, or The Bon-Vivant's Companion*, as a man whose name is "sufficient guarantee" for perfection in the education of how to mix drinks. In his short chapter called "The Cocktail and the Crusta," Thomas states, "The 'Cocktail' is a modern invention, and is generally used on fishing and other sporting parties, although some *patients* insist that it is good in the morning as a tonic." He goes on to list just ten cocktail recipes, bitters being the only ingredient common to each drink. One of these cocktails is made to be bottled (presumably for fishing trips). The others include drinks served on the rocks, drinks chilled on ice and strained before serving (straight up), and in the case of two recipes, drinks devoid of any ice whatsoever.

In *Straight Up or On the Rocks, A Cultural History of American Drink*, author William

Grimes cites an editorial letter dating to 1806 that defines a cocktail as being "a stimulating liquor, composed of spirits of any kind, sugar, water, and bitters. . . " The cocktail, then, was probably born around the turn of the eighteenth century, and fifty-some years later, bitters seemed to be the ingredient that continued to define a drink that could carry the name.

In the mid-twentieth century, David Embury, author of *The Fine Art of Mixing Drinks*, was a very well respected authority on mixed drinks and very opinionated when it came to what was and what wasn't a cocktail. In the 1952 edition of his book, Embury stated that cocktails were for pre-prandial consumption only, and as such, they must whet the appetite. He went on to say that cocktails must "please the senses" and that a well-made cocktail "breaks the ice of formal reserve." All this still holds true, though now many drinks more suitable to post-prandial consumption are commonly referred to as cocktails.

These days, if a bartender deems to call a drink a cocktail, then a cocktail it is. A cocktail used to be considered an elegant, sophisticated drink; and most cocktails, even as recently as the 1950s, contained bitters of one sort or another. Now, we see drinks made in test tubes being referred to as cocktails; and bitters, although not forgotten, have been overlooked by many modern-day bartenders. Bitters—be they Angostura, Peychaud, or orange—have historical footings in the life of the cocktail. Our fondest wish is that bartenders of today and tomorrow will once again realize that bitters are perhaps the most important ingredients behind any bar.

What Makes a New Classic?

Will the drinks detailed in this book be poured at bars one hundred years from now? Only time will tell. We considered more than five hundred drinks for this book; and the ones that appear here are, in our opinion, not only the best drinks we tested (although there were others that, space permitting, deserved mention) but also representative of the types of drinks that the drinking public now demands. Not all of these creations are sophisticated Martini-style cocktails, although many fit that category to a tee; but each one of them has been well thought out by the bartender or chef who first made it, and every drink in this book deserves to be recorded for cocktail mavens in the distant future.

Not all of these drinks are brand-spanking new. For example, we have included the Caipirinha, a classic Brazilian drink that has been served in Rio for decades. Still, though, the drink has only recently become popular in the United States, and the Caipirinha is, indeed, a classic. Without it, this book would be incomplete.

We have also included some cocktails that were created by marketers in an attempt to promote their products. In certain cases— the Hennessy Martini is probably the best example—it would have been just plain wrong to omit them. The Hennessy Martini has become very popular in recent years; it's a complex, sophisticated drink that can be ordered at almost any bar, and it will surely be around for many years to come.

The other name-brand quandary we had to attack was this: If a bartender stipulated a certain brand of, say, vodka, in a cocktail, should that brand name appear in the recipe? And here, we have been somewhat subjective. While we didn't want this book to serve as an advertisement for brand-name liquors, the truth is, *some* liquors have no substitute. And although most unflavored vodkas can be substituted one for another in most mixed drinks (the Vodka Martini is the obvious exception), such is not always the case with flavored vodkas or other spirits. Some brand names are mentioned for accuracy: Bradley Ogden's tequila infusion calls for Jose Cuervo Traditionale tequila. It's a drink created especially for that particular bottling; and although another tequila might work very well in this recipe, this Mexican spirit does vary tremendously from one label to the next. The brand name is mentioned in the recipe; you can use whichever tequila you want.

In choosing these drinks, we also had to take into account that whenever a drink becomes popular, variations on the theme will spring up across the country. Sex on the Beach is an excellent example: In the early Eighties, the drink was made from vodka, peach schnapps, orange juice, and cranberry juice. It was a simple affair, and it worked fairly well. These days, however, Sex on the Beach seems to be made according to a different recipe wherever you go. After more than a few years of scouring bars throughout the nation, publications of every stripe, and more recently, the World Wide Web, we have found versions that include amaretto, melon liqueur, cassis, pineapple juice, raspberry liqueur, triple sec, apple schnapps, and even scotch whisky. Moreover, the bartenders who pour these potions will swear that the drink originated in their hometown—anywhere from Hilton Head Island to Seattle—and they will stake their lives on the fact that they were there when the drink was first concocted. The truth has been swept beneath the bar.

The reverse of this phenomenon can also be true: Drinks made from the same exact ingredients are often known by different names in different bars, and it's entirely possible that many of them were created at the same time, by different people. Take, for example, Martini Thyme, a cocktail created by Ted and Linda Fondulas of Hemingway's restaurant in Killington, Vermont. The drink is made with gin and Chartreuse and served in a cocktail glass with a sprig of thyme. It is likely that other bartenders have also combined gin and Chartreuse; maybe they didn't add a sprig of thyme and maybe they gave the drink a different name, but still, the drink would have been very similar. Where noted, these cocktails, as far as we can ascertain, were created by the people to whom we give credit.

How to Make a Drink

Making drinks will be much easier and the results will be far more spectacular if you first learn some basic techniques and invest in the correct utensils and the appropriate ingredients. We have seen bartenders who don't know which side of a lemon twist to point toward the glass, and even a few who think it's okay to merely drop the twist into a drink without releasing its precious oils. But the first job of the day for professional bartenders who take pride in their job is to set up the bar; and whether you are mixing drinks at home or actually earning a living behind the bar, a bit of technique and organization will smooth the way.

Building Drinks

The term *build* is used in connection with drinks that are poured straight into an ice-filled glass and stirred together, usually with a stirrer or straw that remains in the drink when it is served. Unless the recipe calls for a "floater," which should not be mixed in—such as the Galliano that floats on top of a Harvey Wallbanger—you should add all of the ingredients before stirring the drink.

The ingredient measures in this book are called for in ounces. If you're unfamiliar with ounce measures, here's a handy ounce to tablespoon/cup conversion chart.

$^1/_2$ ounce = 1 tablespoon = 3 teaspoons

1 ounce = 2 tablespoons

2 ounces = 4 tablespoons = $^1/_4$ cup

3 ounces = 6 tablespoons

4 ounces = $^1/_2$ cup

Shaking Drinks

As a general rule, drinks made with fruit juices, milk, and/or cream should be shaken before serving; but there are exceptions: The Screwdriver is a *built* drink. For shaking drinks, use a professional Boston shaker (a two-part affair with a metal cup and a glass cup that fit inside each other to contain the ingredients) or choose a cocktail shaker with a lid and built-in strainer. You should always shake a drink vigorously and for a relatively short time: five to ten seconds. This will chill your drink sufficiently without diluting it too much. Remember, however, that a certain amount of water, melted from the ice cubes, is integral to most cocktails.

If the drink you are making is to be served over ice, strain it into a glass full of fresh ice cubes; never simply pour the drink, partially melted cubes and all, into an empty glass. On the other hand, if you are serving the drink straight up (without ice) you should chill the glass before adding the cocktail (see "Chilling Glasses," at right).

Stirring Drinks

Clear drinks, such as the Martini and Manhattan, should be stirred over ice before being served. James Bond, of course, would disagree; he liked his Martinis "shaken, not stirred." However, we are adamant about this procedure. We believe—some would say foolishly—that when a bartender lovingly stirs a cocktail, a procedure that should take between 20 and 30 seconds, he or she has a moment to reflect. After a little practice, a good bartender knows exactly when the drink is ready to be poured. As with shaken drinks, if the cocktail is going to be served over ice, use fresh ice in the glass, and if the drink is of the straight-up variety, chill the glass thoroughly before straining the cocktail.

You can stir drinks in a Martini pitcher with a spout that catches the ice and negates the need for a strainer, or in a mixing glass (the glass half of a Boston shaker). Martini pitchers usually come with their own glass stirrers, but you'll need a bar spoon—long, slim, with an almost-flat bowl—to stir in a mixing glass.

Chilling Glasses

The best chilled glasses come straight from the freezer and acquire an icy coating when they meet warmer air. But if you have no prechilled glasses, here's the best way to cope: Before beginning to assemble the cocktail ingredients, place the glass in the sink, fill it with ice cubes, and add cold water until the water spills over the sides of the glass. Let the glass stand while you prepare the cocktail. When the glass is needed, shake it for about ten seconds so that the ice water spills over the outside of the glass. Pour out the ice and water, take hold of the base of the glass, and shake out any excess water. Don't dry the glass, but do provide a cocktail napkin to catch the moisture.

Layering Drinks

When making a layered drink, the liqueur or liquor with the highest density (specific gravity) should be the first one poured into the glass, followed by the next-highest density, and so forth—that way, the different colored ingredients will form layers that actually float one atop the other. However, since one brand of, say, sambuca can have a heavier or lighter density than another brand, experience, an eye for viscosity, and trial and error will be your best tutors. After pouring the first liquor into a short, slim pousse-café glass, each successive liquor should be poured over the back of a small spoon so that the liquor drizzles gently, rather than pours, onto the preceding liquor.

Rimming Glasses

Nothing upsets us more than a Margarita glass that is encrusted, inside and out, with salt. (Ditto the cocoa powder on a Chocolate Martini and the mixture of sugar and orange zest that we use on a Cosmopolitan.) These ingredients are meant to be a treat for the drinker's mouth and palate, not an ingredient that melts down the inside of the glass into the cocktail. Therefore, no matter what you have seen or heard, never upend the rim of the glass into a saucer or bowl that's been mounded with salt or other ingredients. Instead, here is the proper technique: First,

the rim of the glass must be moistened so that the rimming ingredient will adhere to it. Do this by rubbing a wedge of lemon or lime around the outside of the rim or by daubing the outside of the rim with a bit of paper towel that has been dipped in one of the drink's main ingredients. Next, hold the glass sideways—stem to the left, bowl of the glass to the right—over a sheet of waxed paper or the waste basket. Sprinkle the salt (or other ingredient) onto the moistened rim, while turning the stem end, to coat the rim evenly all the way around. After coating the entire rim, use a clean paper towel to remove any ingredient that has fallen into the inside of the glass. (If you pour the rimming ingredient into a salt shaker, spice bottle, or dredger with a perforated top, it's just that much easier.) If you are entertaining a crowd, glasses can be rimmed hours ahead of time; just set the glasses aside, out of harm's way.

Preparing Garnishes

Fruit wedges, such as limes or lemons, are easy to prepare. First, wash the fruit: Who knows where it's been. Remove both ends of the fruit, and then slice it in half around the center or from top to bottom. Next, cut each half into four equal wedges. When adding a wedge of fruit as a garnish, remember that it is also an ingredient; the juice should be squeezed from the fruit before you add it to the drink.

Twists, usually made from lemons, limes, or oranges, are prepared by removing the stem end from the fruit to give it a flat base to stand on. Place the fruit upright on a cutting board. Using a sharp paring knife and working from top to bottom, cut $1/2$-inch-wide strips of zest that incorporate some but not much of the white inner pith. To add a twist to a drink: Hold it, colored-side down, about two inches above the surface of the drink. Gently twist it to release the oils from the zest onto the top of the drink, and then rub the colored side of the twist around the rim of the glass. Finally, gently drop the twist into the drink.

To prepare wheels or slices of fruit, first remove both ends from the fruit, cutting deep enough to expose the pulp. For wheels, cut the fruit into thin slices. If desired, cut each wheel into a half-wheel. To hang a wheel or slice over the rim of the glass, cut through the peel and halfway into the pulp; use this slit to fit the fruit over the lip of the glass.

Glassware

Good-quality, thin-rimmed, sophisticated glassware boosts any drinking experience. All of the drinks in this book call for specific styles of glasses for serving; and when possible, you should stick to each bartender's choice of glass. When a "cocktail" glass is called for, this refers to the sleek, stemmed glass with a V-shaped bowl that's often referred to as a Martini glass. You'll also find references to old-fashioned and double old-fashioned glasses (the latter usually has almost twice the capacity of the former), which are normally wide-mouthed, stemless glasses that will hold six to ten ounces. Rocks glasses are similar to old-fashioned glasses, though they sometimes are stemmed. Highball glasses generally hold eight to twelve ounces of liquid; and collins glasses are tall, thin, and stemless, usually

between ten and fourteen ounces in capacity. Goblets and wineglasses can be used for many of the cocktails included here.

Bar Ingredients

Sometimes it's the little things, the ones that add the finishing touches, that are most important to a drink. A few ingredients are key to producing many of the older classic cocktails and lots of the new drinks contained in this book. Make sure your bar is stocked with the following (for mail-order sources, see page 131): Angostura, Peychaud, and orange bitters; maraschino cherries; sugar cubes and granulated sugar; coarse salt; grenadine (look for a bottle that states it was made from pomegranates; many bottlings are merely red sugar water); and lime juice cordial (such as the products made by Rose's or Angostura).

Although lime juice cordials are necessary to make drinks such as the Gimlet, recipes for drinks such as the Margarita are correct only when freshly squeezed lime juice is used. Similarly, although some bars persist in using premade "sweet and sour mix," you will find that the use of freshly squeezed lemon juice (or lime juice) with a touch of simple syrup added will result in far better cocktails. And, of course (with the exception of cranberry juice, which is not palatable straight from the berry), you should try to use fresh fruit juices whenever possible.

One bar ingredient worth making and keeping on hand is simple syrup. It can make the difference between a so-so cocktail and one that's perfection itself; and although many bartenders use superfine "bar" sugar, we generally prefer (exceptions are noted) to use simple syrup. Making simple syrup is quick and easy, plus it will keep indefinitely if stored in the refrigerator. An added bonus is that it's useful in cooking: Add some to pureed berries for a quick sorbet and use it for sweetening cold liquids.

SIMPLE SYRUP
makes 2³/₄ cups

2 cups granulated sugar

2 cups water

1. In a small saucepan, combine the sugar with the water. Cook over moderate heat, stirring occasionally, until the sugar completely dissolves and the syrup is clear, 3 to 6 minutes. Do not boil. Remove the pan from the heat and allow the syrup to cool.

2. Pour the simple syrup into a bottle or jar. Refrigerate the syrup; it will keep indefinitely. We recommend that you store the syrup in a bottle fitted with a professional pour spout.

The Cocktails

THE AÑEJO HIGHBALL

Created by Dale DeGroff, beverage manager at Rainbow, New York City
(see also the International Cocktail, page 57)

Dale DeGroff is proof positive that bartending is a craft, not a job. His ardent study and research, his attention to historical precedent, and his enthusiasm for his work make him the equal of the world's finest gourmet chefs. And just like any good restaurateur, Dale understands that dealing with customers in an amiable manner is as important to his success as the most pristine mixology techniques. In fact, he learned how to get along with people from bartender Mike O'Connor (currently behind the bar at Hurley's in Manhattan) while serving food at the original Charley O's in New York City, quite a few years before he learned how to mix a drink.

"I was a waiter at Charley O's in the mid-Seventies," recalls Dale, "and they had the contract to cater special functions at the mayor's residence, Gracie Mansion. One day, they were really stuck for a bartender, and I volunteered for the job. I scribbled down a few drink recipes on a scrap of paper and bluffed my way through the evening. After that, I became the regular bartender for Mayor Abe Beame."

Dale moved to Los Angeles in 1978 and became a bartender at the Hotel Bel-Air, where he learned "finesse"; but it wasn't until one of his drinking buddies, an older bartender from the Hermitage in Los Angeles, taught him how to construct a Between the Sheets cocktail that he finally understood that it was imperative to learn how to make drinks in the classic mode. "I used to use sweet-and-sour mix and American brandy in my Between the Sheets," he says, grimacing a bit when he reveals this. "But this old-time bartender—I hate to admit it, but I can't recall his name—showed me that if you use fresh lemon juice and French cognac and then dust the rim of the glass with a little powdered sugar, you can make a drink of which to be proud."

Returning to New York in 1985, Dale looked up an old acquaintance, legendary restaurateur Joe Baum. The two met in the early Seventies, when Joe was president of Restaurant Associates and Dale was working for the advertising agency that handled the company's account. (Before that, he had worked as a dishwasher at the Times Square location of Howard Johnson's and had served a brief spell packaging Bibles on 23rd Street.) In short order, Dale was hired as head bartender at Joe Baum's

Aurora restaurant in 1985; and then in 1987, he took the same position at Rainbow, the complex atop the GE Building in Rockefeller Center that encompasses the Rainbow Room, Rainbow and Stars, and the Promenade Bar.

Rainbow is the New York City location of your dreams: The view of the Manhattan skyline is sublime; the service, exquisite; the glassware, sleek and stylish; and the art deco decor, strictly top-notch 1930s chic. Elegance abounds, you forget the hustle and bustle of the city streets, and for a few hours you can view the modern world from above—way above—the crowd. Take your choice from the cocktails on the menu: All are exquisitely crafted, and although Dale no longer graces the far side of the mahogany, his influence can be seen in every last detail of the drinks and the service at Rainbow.

Dale's Añejo Highball is his tribute to the great Cuban bartenders who created impeccable cocktails during Havana's heyday of the Twenties and Thirties. "This drink," says Dale, "merges a mixture of ingredients that, in my opinion, displays how necessary it is for bartenders to understand each and every ingredient in a drink. I consider this to be a spicy drink, full of big flavors; and the bitters brings them all together in complete harmony."

THE AÑEJO HIGHBALL
makes 1 cocktail

1 1/2 ounces añejo rum

1/2 ounce orange curaçao

1/2 ounce freshly squeezed lime juice

2 dashes Angostura bitters

4 to 5 ounces ginger beer

1 lime wheel and 1 orange slice, for garnishes

Fill an 8- to 12-ounce highball glass with ice cubes. Add all of the ingredients; stir briefly, just to blend. Hook the citrus garnishes over the rim of the glass or float them on top. Serve at once.

THE AWOL
makes 1 cocktail

$1/2$ ounce melon liqueur
$1/2$ ounce chilled pineapple juice
$1/2$ ounce vodka
$1/2$ ounce 151-proof rum

1. Layer the ingredients, one at a time, in a 2-ounce pousse-café glass.

2. Carefully ignite the rum and allow it to burn for only 7 to 10 seconds. Extinguish the flame by blowing it out or covering the top with the stem of another glass.

3. When you are certain that the flame is extinguished, follow Lane's instructions very carefully: Drink slowly in one luxurious swallow.

THE AWOL

Created for a Smirnoff vodka cocktail competition in 1993 by Lane Zellman while bartender at the Louis XVI restaurant in the St. Louis Hotel, New Orleans

In the late 1700s, bourbon floated down the Mississippi from Kentucky to New Orleans on flatboats. In 1976, Lane and Susan Zellman floated down the Mississippi from Minnesota to New Orleans on a houseboat. Bourbon became responsible for a street name in the Big Easy; and Lane is responsible for creating the AWOL, a pyrotechnic pousse-café-style shooter.

When Lane arrived in New Orleans, armed with a B.A. in English literature, he took a bartending job at Houlihan's on Bourbon Street. "I love tending bar so much," he says, smiling, "that it has become my career—and Susan's. She tends bar at the Royal Sonesta Hotel."

After working at Houlihan's for five years, during which time he became the bar manager, Lane moved on to the mahogany at the Fairmont Hotel, where he found a major treasure—a bar book full of cocktail recipes from the 1930s. "There were many pousse-café-style drinks in there," recalls Lane. "And when business was slow, I experimented with them."

The one bartending technique that he had never really mastered, however, was pouring the liquors over the back of a spoon, an essential part of layering pousse-cafés. But Lane discovered that if he held a maraschino cherry by the stem and poured the liquors over the cherry, the effect was the same: The cherry broke the fall of the spirit and the drink layered, each ingredient on top of the last, quite nicely.

Lane now works at Michael's Mid-City Grill, a neighborhood restaurant on Canal Street in New Orleans; but it was while he was tending bar at the Louis XVI restaurant, in the St. Louis Hotel, that he created the AWOL. This shooter—a layered creation with style and finesse—is truly a classic drink: The warm, high-proof rum is the first thing to slide down your throat, followed quickly by the mouth-cleansing shot of vodka and then the dash of chilled pineapple juice. Finally, there's a soothing tot of melon liqueur that lingers pleasantly in the mouth. The AWOL—Absence (of brain) without Leave, according to its creator—was originally created with Midori liqueur and Smirnoff vodka (no brand name was noted for the rum), but you should feel free to use whatever bottlings you wish.

THE BLOOD ORANGE

Created in 1995 by John Simmons, of Petaluma restaurant in New York City, with influence from Bob Camillone, of the Paddington Corp. A similar but slightly different version was created simultaneously by Molly Lynch, brand manager for Campari.

Carl Jung had his theory of synchronicity, but we think the origin of this drink is less cosmic than all that. We think that a good idea is a good idea and that this type of simultaneous inventiveness is on the rise, especially when we're talking about smart people who know their subject. Here's the scenario: A new product hits the market—in this case, Stolichnaya Ohranj vodka—and creative bartenders immediately start playing around with it. Campari, the bitter Italian spirit, is wildly popular; and lo and behold! total strangers put these ingredients together and come up with the same drink.

One creator of the Blood Orange is native New Yorker John Simmons, bartender since 1988 at Petaluma, an Italian restaurant on Manhattan's Upper East Side. One day, while experimenting behind the bar and passing some time with Bob Camillone, representative of the Paddington Corp. (liquor importers), John hit upon the idea for this drink. "One of my favorite drinks is Campari and vodka," says John, "and when Stolichnaya Ohranj hit the market, I simply put the two ingredients together to see what would happen."

But he's flexible in his presentation. "I see the drink as a hybrid," he says. "You can serve it as a cocktail—straight up in a Martini glass, on the rocks, or in a highball glass with club soda."

Bob Camillone, excited about John's new drink, took the recipe to Molly Lynch, brand manager for Campari, one of Paddington's imports. Imagine his surprise when Molly had already mixed the two ingredients. "It was just a natural match," says Molly. "As soon as Stolichnaya Ohranj hit the market, I thought of marrying it with Campari, since Campari and orange juice is a classic combination."

Molly's version calls for a fifty-fifty mix of Campari and Stolichnaya Ohranj, served in a Martini glass with a splash of club soda; John's creation favors two parts vodka to one part Campari, garnished with a slice of blood orange.

You should feel free to mix the Blood Orange in whatever proportion suits your palate; use more Campari and a splash of club soda for Molly's version or serve it in any one of the three ways John suggests.

THE BLOOD ORANGE
makes 1 cocktail

3 ounces Stolichnaya Ohranj vodka

$1^1/_2$ ounces Campari

Club soda, if serving as a highball

1 blood orange slice, for garnish (optional)

To serve straight up: Fill a large mixing glass two-thirds full of ice cubes.
Add the vodka and Campari; stir until well blended and chilled.
Strain into a chilled cocktail glass. Garnish, if desired.

To serve on the rocks: Fill a double old-fashioned glass with ice.
Add the vodka and Campari and stir to blend. Garnish, if desired.

To serve as a highball: Fill a 10- to 12-ounce highball glass with ice.
Pour in the ingredients and add club soda to taste; stir to blend.
Garnish, if desired.

BOLO'S SANGRIAS: POMEGRANATE AND WHITE PEACH

Created by Bobby Flay, chef-owner of Bolo, New York City.

Bobby Flay must be the coolest celebrity chef in the country. Complete with flaming red hair, dark shades, and an impish grin, Bobby turns out Southwestern food at New York's Mesa Grill and Spanish cuisine at Bolo; and all of the dishes he serves have a certain twist that has become Bobby's impressive signature. In 1993, he was voted Rising Star Chef of the Year by the James Beard Foundation, and he also garnered the French Culinary Institute's Outstanding Graduate Award. But despite his stardom and his outwardly cool demeanor, Bobby has remained not just approachable but a downright friendly guy. When he was about to open his third restaurant, Mesa City, we asked him about his other aspirations. "I wanna play more golf," he said with a grin.

Bobby's genius for flavors has spilled over from the sauté pans in the kitchen to the glasses at the bar. Although he shies away from creating completely original cocktails, he brings his own flavors to drinks, such as the two sangrias served at Bolo. "When I see an ingredient that can be utilized in a cocktail," he says, "I try to put it to use at the bar. We can now buy pomegranate molasses and white peach puree even when the fruits are out of season, so I used these products to make my own sangrias. We offer both red and white versions of this traditional Spanish drink so that customers can order them to drink alongside almost any dish on the menu."

If you can't find pomegranate molasses, pomegranate juice is available in many specialty food stores, and if white peach puree isn't available in your neck of the woods, simply pop some slices of ripe peach (preferably white, but if not available, use the regular variety) into the blender and whirr until the mixture is smooth. But whatever you do, don't miss out on trying these spectacularly refreshing drinks. If you have never tasted Bobby Flay's food, these sangrias will show you what all the fuss is about.

BOLO'S POMEGRANATE SANGRIA
makes 8 to 10 servings

One 750-ml bottle dry red wine

1 cup American brandy

1 cup Simple Syrup (page 10)

$^1/_2$ cup freshly squeezed orange juice

$^3/_4$ cup pomegranate molasses or pomegranate juice

2 oranges, cut into thin wheels

3 green apples, cored and thinly sliced

2 lemons, cut into thin wheels

1 cup ice cubes, for serving

1. Combine the wine, brandy, simple syrup, orange juice, pomegranate, and all of the sliced fruits in a pitcher or large bowl; stir to blend well. Cover and refrigerate for at least 2 hours and up to 2 days.

2. Stir in the ice cubes. Ladle or pour the sangria into stemmed glasses, taking care that each portion gets some of the fruit.

BOLO'S WHITE PEACH SANGRIA
makes 8 to 10 servings

One 750-ml bottle Pinot Grigio

1 cup American brandy

1 cup Simple Syrup (page 10)

$^1/_2$ cup freshly squeezed orange juice

$^3/_4$ cup white peach puree

4 ripe peaches, stoned and sliced

3 green apples, cored and thinly sliced

2 lemons, cut into thin wheels

1 cup ice cubes, for serving

1. Combine the wine, brandy, simple syrup, orange juice, peach puree, and all of the sliced fruits in a pitcher or large bowl; stir to blend well. Cover and refrigerate for at least 2 hours and up to 2 days.

2. Stir in the ice cubes. Ladle or pour the sangria into stemmed glasses, taking care that each portion gets some of the fruit.

THE BURNT ORANGE KIR

Created by Ted and Linda Fondulas, owners of Hemingway's restaurant in Killington, Vermont
(see also Martini Thyme, page 77)

Hemingway's is much more of a restaurant than a bar, but, although "new classical" cuisine is the focus at the restored Asa Briggs 1860 house (where Asa is said to have kept a bear for a pet), owners Ted and Linda Fondulas regularly create new cocktails to round out their customers' dining experiences.

Although neither Fondulas claims to be an expert bartender, this recipe shows that they both have the innate ability to know when to stop adding ingredients. The Burnt Orange Kir uses only two spirits, but a third aspect comes into play in the form of its garnish. In this case it's the caramelized orange oils that dot the surface of the cocktail and give the drink an added dimension. When making the Burnt Orange Kir, you should remember that Cynar (chee-NAHR), an apéritif made from artichokes among other things, is rather bitter. Therefore, feel free to alter the ratio of Lillet to Cynar according to your taste.

THE BURNT ORANGE KIR
makes 1 cocktail

4 ounces chilled Lillet Blanc

$1/4$ to $1/2$ ounce Cynar

1 strip of orange peel, about 3 inches long

1. Pour the Lillet and Cynar into a chilled cocktail glass.

2. Light a match and hold it about 3 inches above the surface of the drink. Take the orange peel and carefully twist it between the thumb and forefinger of your other hand. The oils from the orange peel will ignite and fall to rest on the surface of the drink. (This is a somewhat complicated procedure for one person; if need be, ask a friend to hold the match while you twist the orange peel.)

THE CAIPIRINHA

A traditional Brazilian cocktail, origin unknown.

First off, you need to know how to pronounce two Portuguese words: *caipirinha* (kai-purr-EEN-yuh) and *cachaça* (kuh-SHAH-suh). As any beach boy in Rio will tell you, the former is a traditional Brazilian mixed drink, the latter the name of the liquor used to make it. The Caipirinha is Brazil's national drink and has been around for longer than anyone can remember; and yet it deserves a place in this book of new cocktails, simply because only in recent years has the drink gained popularity Stateside. And if ever a drink could be called a classic, the Caipirinha is it.

Roughly translated, the word *caipirinha* means "small country bumpkin" or "hick," possibly because it is prepared and served in the same glass, without straining or any fancy machinations. The Caipirinha requires cachaça, a Brazilian liquor made from raw sugar cane, plus a number of lime wedges and granulated sugar (not superfine sugar or simple syrup) that when muddled helps grind the juice from the citrus pulp and abrade the lime peel so it releases its oils into the drink.

Cachaça often is referred to as "Brazilian rum." And though it might look like light rum and is made from sugar cane, it most definitely doesn't taste like rum at all. While most Caribbean rums are made from the molasses of sugar cane, cachaça comes from unrefined sugar cane; and the resulting product is very, very different: harsher, with a bite that is reminiscent of brandy. Only two brands of cachaça are widely available in the United States, Pitú and Toucano. Pitú is an unaged spirit, somewhat harsh when consumed neat, but it bears full flavors and makes a delicious Caipirinha. Toucano, on the other hand, is designated as a rum and aged in wood for two years, bringing a maturity and complexity not found in the Pitú bottling. Although Toucano lends sophistication to the Caipirinha, a Pitú Caipirinha bears a hearty quality that we adore. Personally, we tend to flit from one bottling to the other, depending on whether we are feeling earthy or refined, at the given moment.

Many recipes for the Caipirinha call for a whole lime, but we believe that they refer to very small Key limes or similar South American varieties. We recommend that you use a sturdy double old-fashioned glass and cut enough wedges (not slices) of lime, to fill the glass to just above the halfway mark; this way the size of the lime is of no consequence. Use a pestle or the back of a very substantial spoon to muddle the limes and sugar together—proper muddling requires pressure, so don't use frail glassware to construct this drink; it just doesn't suit its country bumpkin image.

THE CAIPIRINHA
makes 1 cocktail

Enough lime wedges to half fill a sturdy double old-fashioned glass

2 teaspoons granulated sugar

Crushed ice

2 ounces cachaça

1. Place the lime wedges in a sturdy double old-fashioned glass; sprinkle the sugar over them. Using a pestle or the back of a spoon, muddle the limes and sugar together until the sugar completely dissolves and all of the lime juice is released.

2. Add crushed ice to fill the glass almost to the rim; pour in the cachaça and stir briefly. Serve at once.

THE CAJUN MARTINI

Created in 1980 by Chef Paul Prudhomme and his wife, K,
at K-Paul's Louisiana Kitchen, New Orleans.

The Cajun Martini is the forerunner of all of the modern infused drinks. True, infusions didn't become truly popular until the 1990s, but this drink was the talk of the country almost a decade before American bars were displaying jars, jugs, and decanters filled with fruits, herbs, and spices in, usually, vodka.

How did it all begin? Chef Paul Prudhomme was the first: "The restaurant that inhabited the space we picked for K-Paul's used to be a somewhat, well, raunchy joint; it was a hangout for seafaring families and the place where lots of workers would cash their paychecks at the end of the week," recalls the spiciest chef in New Orleans. "One of our first tasks was to discourage the old clientele from frequenting our restaurant."

Initially, K-Paul's restaurant didn't offer any drinks at all, but after about three months, most of the old regulars had disappeared, and Chef Paul was offering beer to his customers. "Five years later we added after-dinner drinks, beer, and two wines: Red and White (that is exactly the way they read on the menu)."

Presently K-Paul's has a full bar with a wide selection of fine wines and creative drinks.

"A lot of my chef friends used liquor in their food dishes," says Chef Paul, "so I thought it would be interesting to add food to liquor instead. We played around with all sorts of vegetables, but it was my wife, K, who first thought of infusing gin with cayenne peppers. The first bottle of Cajun Martinis lasted a full three months. About a year later I happened to glance at an invoice for more than a few cases of gin and asked K (who ordered the liquor and ran the front of the house) about the order. 'They love our Cajun Martinis,' she said."

And thus the seed of a hot, hot trend was planted.

Many people since that time have elaborated on the Cajun Martini. Chefs and bartenders have created their own versions of the drink by adding an assortment of different varieties of peppers, onions, garlic, and vegetables; and some variations have been quite successful. The original Cajun Martini, however, has that quintes-

sential quality that helps define classic cocktails: simplicity. Gin itself holds a multitude of flavors; many bottlings contain exotic herbs and spices such as coriander, fennel, calamus root, angelica, cardamom, cassia, ginger, cinnamon, licorice, caraway seed, orange and lemon peels, and of course, juniper berries. The addition of just one solitary pepper—jalapeño or cayenne—and a dash of vermouth, serves to add an extra dimension to this drink without detracting completely from the intricacies of the base liquor. Chef Paul makes this drink with either gin or vodka; the vodka version is also a stunning drink but not quite as complex as the gin-based Cajun Martini.

Be sure to follow the instructions very carefully. When we first experimented with this infusion, we removed the top, tail, and seeds from the chile pepper, and the resultant drink was nowhere near as flavorful as the one that will fill your glass when you leave those aspects intact. If the pepper won't fit into the neck of your gin bottle, simply add the vermouth first to get the correct ratio of gin to vermouth; then decant the Martini into a large glass jar, add the pepper, seal, and refrigerate.

CAJUN MARTINIS
makes 5 sizeable cocktails

1 fresh cayenne or jalapeño chile pepper, washed and dried
One 750-ml bottle gin or vodka (use a bottle that has never been opened)
About 1 ounce dry vermouth
Pickled green tomatoes or okra, for garnish (optional)

1. Slice the chile lengthwise, cutting up to but not through the stem, leaving the stem intact and the pepper essentially whole, though sliced. Do not remove the seeds. Push the chile into the liquor bottle.

2. Add enough vermouth to reach all the way up to the lip of the bottle. Reseal the bottle. Refrigerate for at least 8 hours and up to but no more than 16 hours.

3. Line a funnel with a double layer of dampened cheesecloth. Strain the gin or vodka through it into a clean bottle or pitcher. Discard the chile pepper. Pour the infused Martini back into its bottle. Refrigerate until very well chilled.

4. Serve the Martinis at will, poured directly into chilled cocktail glasses. Garnish each drink with a pickled green tomato or other vegetable, if desired.

THE CHAMBORD KAMIKAZE

makes 1 cocktail

3 ounces vodka

$1/2$ ounce triple sec or Cointreau

$1/2$ ounce freshly squeezed lemon juice

$1/2$ ounce Simple Syrup (see page 10)

$1/2$ ounce Chambord

$1/2$ lime, cut into thin wheels

1 lime wheel, for garnish

Fill a large shaker glass two-thirds full of ice cubes. Pour in all of the liquid ingredients; add the sliced lime. Do the Seattle Muddle (see text) for 20 to 30 seconds, or until very well mixed. Strain the liquids into a chilled cocktail glass. Garnish with the lime wheel.

THE CHAMBORD KAMIKAZE

Recipe from Peter Meddick, bartender at the Bookstore Bar and Cafe
in the Alexis Hotel, Seattle.

Peter Meddick doesn't claim to have invented this drink, which has been popular in the Seattle area since the early Nineties. As with many popular drinks, the original creator is lost to history. This particular recipe, however, is the one used by all of the bartenders in this delightfully quirky hotel bar that feels more like a comfortable neighborhood hangout than a tony hotel cocktail lounge. You can actually buy books at the Bookstore Bar, peruse the magazines laid out on an adjacent shelf, nibble on small dishes or have a casual meal (try the wonderful Panini, Italian-style toasted sandwiches), and sip your favorite elixir while being entertained by the bartender or waitperson—all of whom are disarmingly friendly.

So why did we choose this particular recipe for a drink that is made differently all over the country? Mainly because of the way they prepare it at the Bookstore Bar, using a technique that we have never seen outside of Seattle. The Seattle Muddle, as we have dubbed this innovative cocktail-making method, seems to add extra zip to the drink and produces a sharp tanginess that makes this version shine brilliantly above any of the others we tested.

Muddling ingredients for drinks such as the Old-Fashioned is a common sight: The bartender puts some wedges of fresh fruit, a couple of dashes of bitters, and a teaspoon or so of sugar into the glass. Then, a pestle or the back of a sturdy spoon is used to mash the ingredients together, dissolve the sugar, extract the juices, and thoroughly intermingle all of the flavors. Finally, the ice and spirits are added.

In Seattle, however, the bartenders make drinks such as the Chambord Kamikaze by filling a large shaker glass two-thirds full of ice cubes. Next, all of the ingredients (fruit wedges, fruit juices, and the liquors) go in; and finally, the bartender covers the top of the shaker with the palm of his or her hand, slots a wooden pestle into the glass between the thumb and forefinger, and bashes the heck out of the entire drink. The result? Heaven. This muddling method uses the ice cubes as battering rams to release the oils from the citrus peel and the juices from the pulp, still managing to mingle the ingredients well. At the same time, it splinters the ice and chills the mixture very quickly. The drink is then strained into a cocktail glass, garnished, and served immediately. You will notice that a few slivers of ice will make their way into the glass, and this ice keeps the drink chilled for a little longer than a shaken or stirred cocktail. It also creates a sparkling surface on the drink. Though the Seattle Muddle doesn't work with all cocktails, it's the perfect way to make a Chambord Kamikaze.

THE CHILE RITA

Created in 1996 by executive chef David Walzog and general manager Jason Lapin of Tapika, New York City (see also the Tapika Cocktail, page 125).

"*When executive chef* David Walzog and I were designing the beverage program for Tapika, we thought carefully about what type of drinks people enjoyed with David's full-flavored Southwestern food. The fact is, many people drink beer or cocktails with this type of cuisine, so we decided that we should elevate our array of beers and mixed drinks to the same high qualities that we insist on for our wine list," says Jason Lapin, co-creator of the Chile Rita.

Chef Walzog notes that since nobody knows the flavors of the food in any restaurant better than the chef, "Who's better to create drinks to complement the menu?"

The Chile Rita found life when these two ardent restaurateurs wanted to adorn the bar with an infused tequila; the color of this infusion, a wonderful greenish yellow shade, is a real eye-catcher. They simply made a Margarita using jalapeño-infused Sauza Conmemorativo tequila, and a star was born. David suggests that the Chile Rita makes a wonderful accompaniment to his red meat dishes because, he explains, "It marries extremely well with the 'bloody flavors' of steak."

Since the jalapeños really become the predominant flavor in the Chile Rita, you might want to substitute your favorite bottling of tequila for the Sauza Conmemorativo, but if you are going to buy a bottle specifically to make this drink, stick to the Sauza: Why argue with the pros? This drink sells so quickly at Tapika that they just keep topping off their decanter until the jalapeños lose their bite, at which point they start all over again. For home use, however, we suggest that you strain the tequila from the jalapeños as soon as it's hot enough for your taste buds.

THE CHILE RITA
makes 1 cocktail

Coarse salt, to coat the rim of the glass
$2^1/_2$ ounces Chile Tequila Infusion (recipe below)
$^3/_4$ ounce triple sec
1 ounce freshly squeezed lime juice
1 lime wedge, for garnish

1. Moisten the outside of the rim of a cocktail glass with a wedge of lime or some of the infusion; sprinkle lightly but evenly with the salt (see page 8).

2. Fill a large shaker glass two-thirds full of ice cubes. Add the infusion, triple sec, and lime juice and shake to blend. Strain into the prepared glass; garnish with the lime wedge.

CHILE TEQUILA INFUSION
makes about 24 ounces

One 750-ml bottle Sauza Conmemorativo tequila
15 whole jalapeño chile peppers, washed and dried

1. Pour the tequila into a large glass container with a tight-fitting lid. Add the jalapeños and stir briefly. Close the container and set aside away from direct sunlight for 2 to 5 days. Taste the tequila periodically to judge when it is spicy enough for your taste.

2. Line a funnel with a double layer of dampened cheesecloth. Pour the tequila through it into a clean bottle or pitcher. Discard the jalapeños. Pour the Chile Tequila Infusion back into its bottle. Store indefinitely at room temperature or refrigerated.

THE CHOCOLATE MARTINI
makes 1 cocktail

Unsweetened cocoa powder, to coat the rim of the glass
1 Hershey's Hug candy, unwrapped
2 ounces high-quality vodka
1 1/2 ounces high-quality white crème de cacao

1. Use a few drops of crème de cacao to moisten the outside of the rim of a cocktail glass. Sprinkle lightly but evenly with the cocoa powder. Place the Hershey's Hug, pointed top up, in the bottom of the glass.

2. Fill a large mixing glass two-thirds full of ice cubes. Pour in the vodka and crème de cacao and stir until very well chilled. Strain into the prepared cocktail glass. Serve at once.

THE CHOCOLATE MARTINI

Created in 1993 under the supervision of Kerry Simon, executive chef at Mercury (formerly Max's South Beach), Miami.

"*I'm really sorry.* I just can't remember the name of the bartender who created this drink," says Chef Kerry Simon, "but I often come up with a concept for a cocktail and hand it over to the bar staff."

The Chocolate Martini was a result of just such an occasion, and Max's South Beach was the first restaurant to make the drink. Just like Max's South Beach, Kerry says that Mercury (about to open at the time of writing) will be on the cutting edge of both food and drinks. It will offer modern American food, defined by Kerry as traditional American fare, but lighter, and with more interesting flavors. And under his supervision, new drinks are bound to be created there.

Kerry started his culinary career at Little Caesars Pizza, and the company obviously inspired him. He went on to graduate from the Culinary Institute of America, took an apprenticeship in France, and eventually became the youngest American executive chef at New York's Plaza Hotel. Then he headed south to work at Max's South Beach. As for the chefs-creating-drinks phenomenon, Kerry has a theory: "Chefs are normally partial to a few drinks after a shift in the kitchen," he says. "It makes sense that they would use their creativity to make some concoctions of their own."

The Chocolate Martini is an astounding drink. The ingredients are simple, but the result is a heavenly chocolate cocktail with a very clever garnish. We recommend that you use the finest (in this case, usually the most expensive) crème de cacao you can find to make this drink well.

The original recipe contained 1 1/2 ounces of vodka and 1 ounce of crème de cacao; we have altered the proportions slightly to properly fill our oversized cocktail glasses.

THE CINNABAR NEGRONI
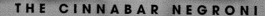
makes 1 cocktail

2 ounces Campari
1 ounce London dry gin
1 ounce sweet vermouth
2 dashes of orange bitters
1 orange slice, for garnish

Fill a double old-fashioned glass with ice cubes.
Add the Campari, gin, and vermouth; sprinkle the bitters
on top. Stir well. Garnish with the orange slice. Serve at once.

THE CINNABAR NEGRONI

Created in 1995 by Jason MacDonald, head bartender at Cinnabar restaurant, Los Angeles.

"*My boss, Alvin Simon,* is a Campari addict," says Jason MacDonald, "and so are many of our customers at Cinnabar. We must be the only restaurant in Los Angeles that orders it by the case."

Apparently, Alvin Simon tends to goad Jason into creating new cocktails with a Campari base, and the Cinnabar Negroni is a direct result of his prodding—not that Jason is new to creating cocktails.

After tending bar in New York City for a few years, Jason moved to Los Angeles in 1991 and found himself a job behind the bar of the Duplex, where he was encouraged to experiment with drinks. "It was around that time that I found a copy of a 1939 cocktail book called *Just Cocktails*, and I started to re-create some of the drinks I found and to use others as a guideline to create variations of my own."

The Cinnabar Negroni is, of course, a variation on a classic drink, the Negroni, that calls for equal parts of Campari, gin, and sweet vermouth. The main differences between the original and Jason's version are that he uses two parts of Campari to one part each of gin and vermouth and he adds orange bitters, which can be somewhat hard to find. Personally, we had such a hard time finding orange bitters that we developed our own recipe before we came across Fee Brothers of Rochester, New York, who make a wonderful version of this age-old ingredient as well as mint bitters, peach bitters, and old-fashioned aromatic bitters (see "Mail-Order Sources," page 131).

With the double-shot of Campari plus the orange bitters, this version of the Negroni takes on a whole new identity. It's delightfully aromatic and refreshing, while at the same time retaining its status as a serious, well-crafted cocktail. Serve it as an apéritif or at any time you want to while away a couple of hours with friends.

THE CITRUS COOLER

Created by Paul Bolles-Beaven, managing partner at
Union Square Cafe, New York City.

Before moving to the Big Apple and gaining employment behind the bar at Union Square Cafe, the only bartending experience that Paul Bolles-Beaven had under his belt came from a few months at a bowling alley in Rhode Island. Now he's a managing partner at one of the nation's top restaurants. Paul gives much credit for his success to his mentor, Danny Meyer, the man who opened Union Square Cafe, hired him, promoted him to the position of wine director after a few short years, and finally made him a co-owner. Indeed, we're fond of quoting Danny, who, when asked by *Nation's Restaurant News* if fine dining were dead, said, "No. Pretentious dining is dead."

Danny is the kind of restaurateur who moves calmly and unobtrusively around the dining room to make sure his guests are happy and hardly ever leaves a table without discreetly removing an empty glass or anything else that his superb waitstaff (truly among the best we have ever seen) hasn't yet seen.

While behind the bar, Paul had an acute appreciation for the creative process. He tinkered with many cocktails and mixed drinks, but none of his creations has endured as well as the Citrus Cooler he created in the early 1990s. "I must admit that several of my drinks barely lasted a week," says Paul, "but many of our regular customers still drink my Citrus Coolers."

Somehow, we don't find that hard to believe at all. Paul used the popular combination of Campari mixed with orange juice and then took it to new heights. It is an adult drink with layers and layers of flavors.

Paul was sampling Aranciata, a tart orange soft drink made by San Pellegrino, when he hit on the concept for the Citrus Cooler. He simply mixed it with a healthy shot of Campari, added some fresh lime juice, and the drink was born. "You can substitute Orangina if you can't find Aranciata," says Paul, "but don't use an overly sweet orange soda." For those who want to try this drink without the alcohol, Paul also created a nonalcoholic version of the Citrus Cooler by using San Pellegrino's Bitter soft drink instead of the Campari. Bitter comes in three-ounce bottles and is available at specialty food stores. It doesn't taste exactly like Campari, but it's similar in flavor. The nonalcoholic version works very well indeed.

We recommend that you serve the Citrus Cooler during the warmer months, but the drink also works very well as an apéritif or even as an accompaniment to brunch at any time of year. Whenever you serve it, we guarantee that your guests will marvel at the intricacies of this simple concoction.

THE CITRUS COOLER
makes 1 cocktail

1¹/₂ ounces Campari

¹/₄ ounce freshly squeezed lime juice

4 ounces Aranciata or Orangina

Fill a collins glass with ice cubes. Add all of the ingredients and stir to blend.
Serve at once.

THE COSMOPOLITAN

Creator unknown.

The Cosmopolitan is probably the most widely known cocktail of these new classics; and although we have tried, for years, to locate its creator, he or she has eluded us. A distinguished writer at *The New York Times* first put us on the scent of a certain Cheryl Cook, reportedly a bartender in Miami. He didn't know anything but her name, having tried to locate her himself. Next, we called the good folks at Cointreau, who claim that the original recipe contained their fine product. They, too, had heard of Cheryl Cook, but had been unable to find her: "Last we heard, she was tending bar in San Francisco."

We have searched high and low for dear Cheryl Cook: We have posted notes on the Internet, called everyone we know in Miami and San Francisco, and scoured telephone directories. We even made a plea in *Food Arts* magazine for Cheryl to contact us; and Ray Foley, publisher of *Bartender* magazine, repeated the same in his publication. If Cheryl Cook exists, she must not want to be found.

Breakthrough: An article by Whitney Walker in the April 10, 1996, edition of New York's *Daily News* claimed that in 1988, New York bartenders Toby Cecchini and Melissa Huffsmith created the version of the Cosmopolitan that contains Absolut Citron vodka.

Disappointment: The Rainbow Room's Dale DeGroff noted that he had drunk of such a potion in San Francisco before Cecchini and Huffsmith created their drink.

Resolution: Let it be said that the Cosmopolitan was created by Bacchus himself, for the truth might never be known.

If you analyze the Cosmopolitan, you'll see that it includes a standard liquor base, Cointreau (or triple sec), a citrus juice, and a dash of cranberry juice. Does this sound familiar? The drink is a vodka-based variation on the Margarita (with cranberry juice added), which, according to a friend of ours known only as "Dr. Cocktail," is a variation on the Sidecar (brandy, Cointreau, and lemon juice). So, in the Cosmopolitan, we have a natural-born classic created, perhaps unwittingly, from two other classic cocktails.

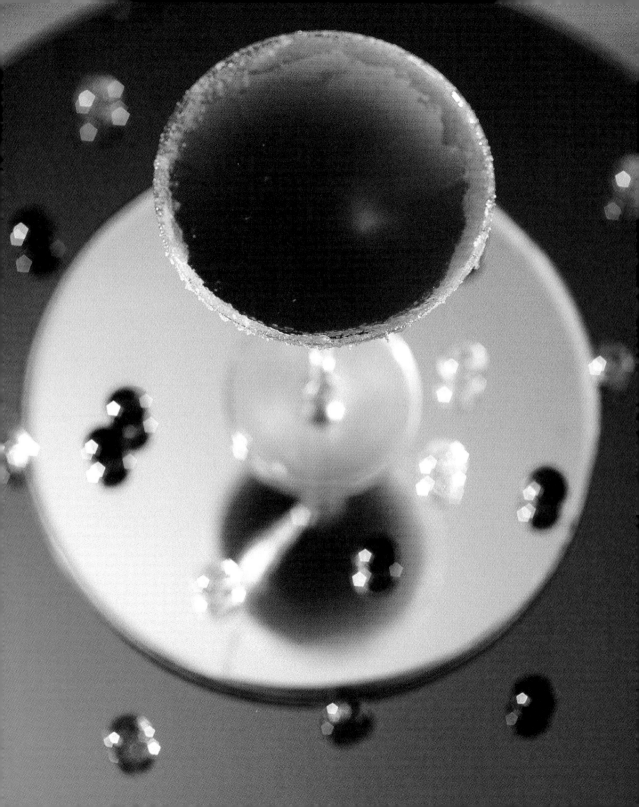

This Cosmopolitan recipe is the result of our own experimentation; and although we are sure that thousands of bartenders use the same, or very similar formulas, we think that rimming the glass with our mix of sugar and orange zest makes a noticeable and very tasty difference.

THE COSMOPOLITAN
makes 1 cocktail

2 teaspoons granulated sugar, to coat the rim of the glass

1 teaspoon finely grated orange zest, to coat the rim of the glass

2 ounces citrus-flavored vodka or unflavored vodka

1 ounce Cointreau

1/2 ounce freshly squeezed lime juice

1/2 ounce Simple Syrup (see page 10)

1 ounce cranberry juice

1. Mix together the sugar and orange zest. Moisten the outside of the rim of a cocktail glass with vodka or lime juice; sprinkle lightly but evenly with the sugar and zest mixture (see page 8).

2. Fill a large shaker glass two-thirds full of ice cubes. Add the vodka, Cointreau, lime juice, simple syrup, and cranberry juice; shake until well blended and chilled. Strain into the prepared glass.

Serve at once.

THE DEBONAIR
makes 1 cocktail

1 ounce Original Canton Delicate Ginger Liqueur
2$\frac{1}{2}$ ounces Oban or Springbank single-malt scotch
1 lemon twist

Fill a large mixing glass two-thirds full of ice cubes. Add the liqueur and scotch and stir until well chilled. Strain into a chilled cocktail glass; garnish with the lemon twist.

THE DEBONAIR

Our creation, 1993.

Here's one of our own inventions; and although it hasn't yet become immensely popular, we have been serving this drink to our friends for nigh on three years—and they keep coming back for more. In fact, Rainbow in New York City added it to their cocktail menu in 1997, and we hope that scotch lovers everywhere give this drink a try.

The Debonair was created with the Whisky Mac in mind. So what, exactly, is a Whisky Mac? In the days when a gin and tonic was just about the most exotic drink to cross the mahogany in Britain (we're talking about the 1960s), some older drinkers used to sip on Whisky Macs, a drink made with blended scotch and ginger wine. It was served neat—no ice, no garnish, no nothing—and although Brits aren't usually known as cocktail fanciers, many of them swore by their Whisky Macs. (Ginger wine is not a wine in the traditional sense of the word, but an infusion of ginger, fruit peels, and spices that has been made in Scotland since the 1700s.)

In the early 1990s, when the Original Canton Delicate Ginger Liqueur was introduced to the United States, we harked back to the Whisky Mac and started experimenting with Canton and various bottlings of scotch. Our goal was to create a new cocktail, but we also had a secondary mission: To take the stuffiness out of single-malt scotch. We are lovers of single malts and usually enjoy them as they should be enjoyed: at room temperature with just a drop of spring water. But why should we enjoy the full flavors of single malts only when we want straight whisky? Blended scotches are perfect for mixing into cocktails, but certain drinks are far better when made with a single malt. Have you ever tasted a Rob Roy made with a good Highland single malt? It's a perfect union of scotch and sweet vermouth.

Thus we embarked on the malt whisky trail, trying to find the perfect bottling to marry to Canton ginger liqueur. We found two: Springbank, a distinguished Campbeltown malt with a crisp bite of sea air that mixed deliciously with Canton, and Oban, a very complex malt from the Western Highlands that bears some of the same briny characteristics as the Springbank (a little more subdued, but with other, more complex flavors that make this one of our all-time favorite bottlings).

THE GREEN FLASH

makes 1 cocktail

$3/4$ ounce melon liqueur

$3/4$ ounce light rum

2 ounces freshly squeezed lime juice

4 ounces guanabana nectar (available in cans
at many supermarkets and specialty food stores)

1 lime wheel, for garnish

Fill a zombie glass or other large glass with ice cubes.
Pour in the liqueur, rum, lime juice, and nectar. Stir with
a straw until chilled. Garnish with the lime wheel.

THE GREEN FLASH

Created by the opening staff of the Four Seasons Resort in Nevis, British West Indies.

We aren't fans of very many tropical drinks. The Piña Colada, when well-crafted, is a delicious classic, and Daiquiris can be exquisite, but most other tropical drinks seem merely a conglomeration of rums and fruit juices thrown together in the hope that the gods of Polynesia or the Caribbean will smile on the creator. And, usually, the result is, well, decent. Oh, sure, there's nothing quite as good as a huge glass full of fruit flavors and a tot of rum to cool you off on a scorching day, but there seems to be neither rhyme nor reason behind the choice of ingredients in most drinks of this ilk. The Green Flash is an exception.

When the sky is crystal clear, sunset on Nevis, sister island to St. Kitts in the Leewards of the British West Indies, can be a magical time. And if you are very lucky and have chosen one of the special days, you will see it: a brilliant green flash that appears in the sky just when the glowing sun sinks into the sea. At that rare moment, you can consider yourself blessed with good fortune by *Nuestra Señora de las Nieves* (Our Lady of the Snows), for whom the island was named by Christopher Columbus. Local folklore claims that a poor Nevisian bachelor once saw the green flash and soon was blessed with a wife, ten children, and a prosperous farm.

When the Four Seasons Resort opened on Nevis in 1991, the bartenders collaborated to create a drink named after the mystical green flash; and this drink, a nectar fit for the gods, is a tribute to this team of bartenders. The Green Flash is a somewhat simple drink, but the guanabana nectar blends beautifully with the other ingredients to make a magnificent cocktail.

HARPER CRANBERRY
makes 1 cocktail

2 ounces I. W. Harper bourbon
3 ounces cranberry juice

Fill a double old-fashioned glass with ice cubes.
Add the bourbon and cranberry juice and stir until chilled.
Serve at once.

HARPER CRANBERRY

Created in 1996 by Kenji Tachihara at the D-Heartman bar in Tokyo.

Okay, here's the strangest-seeming drink in this collection. Bourbon and cranberry juice are an odd combination, but no matter how much you shake your head, there's no denying that this drink works.

The Japanese, generally speaking, love, adore, and are just wild about bourbon. There are bourbon bars in Japan—only bourbons are served—and, of course, the clientele are very conversant in the various brand names and different bottlings. This cocktail calls for I. W. Harper bourbon, a medium-full-bodied whiskey that offers a glorious balance of fruit and spices to the palate and has a history that dates to 1872, when I. W. Bernheim went into the whiskey business in Paducah, Kentucky. Bartender Kenji Tachihara decided to mix this elixir with one of the few other beverages indigenous to the United States: cranberry juice. Bourbon and cranberry juice? Yes, just try it; you'll be astounded.

In the warmer months even the most dedicated whiskey drinkers will turn to rum, gin, or vodka in search of a refreshing cocktail, perhaps one mixed with fruit juices and flavored sodas. But this particular drink is refreshing without being too light; and for some strange reason, the cranberry juice seems to bring out a certain smokiness in the bourbon that can't be detected when it's consumed neat. And so it took a Japanese bartender to out-American the Americans. Truth be told, we doubt whether an American bartender would ever have married these ingredients in the first place. Sip this drink on the Fourth of July and raise your glass to Kenji, a man with a little piece of America in his soul.

THE HENNESSY MARTINI
makes 1 cocktail

3 1/2 ounces Hennessy VS cognac
1 teaspoon freshly squeezed lemon juice
1 lemon twist

Fill a mixing glass two-thirds full of ice cubes. Add the cognac
and lemon juice and stir until well blended and chilled.
Strain into a cold cocktail glass; add the lemon twist.

THE HENNESSY MARTINI

Introduced by the Hennessy Company in 1993.

The Hennessy Martini is simplicity itself: cognac with just a teaspoon of lemon juice. According to Patrick Morley Fletcher, an eighth-generation member of the Hennessy family, this wonderfully constructed classic cocktail has its roots in French history. Adding lemon juice to cognac is a French custom that probably dates to the days when cognac was consumed straight off the still. At that point, the spirit is merely an eau-de-vie. It is clear, just like vodka, and it is flavorful; but it hasn't yet experienced the effects that years in Limousin oak will contribute to this most sophisticated of spirits. Since cognac producers didn't begin purposefully aging their products until the late 1700s, the origins of the Hennessy Martini lay at some time prior to that.

But, apparently, the mixture lived on. The cocktail list at the Round Robin Bar in the Willard Intercontinental Hotel in Washington, D.C., recounts a story about the Marquis de Lafayette, a hero in the Revolutionary War and a close friend of George Washington. According to this tale, the marquis returned to the United States in 1826 to help celebrate the fiftieth anniversary of the Declaration of Independence; and on the Fourth of July that year, the Marquis de Lafayette was observed imbibing in an unfamiliar concoction: cognac and lemon juice.

About forty years ago, Hennessy promoted a drink called the Hennessey Gold Cup, a blend of their cognac and orange juice. The occasion was to celebrate the annual race of the same name held at Newbury, the first steeplechase meet of the British racing season. The Hennessy Gold Cup proved to be a noteworthy race, and drink, and was the inspiration for the Hennessy Martini, introduced in 1993.

The official recipe for the Hennessy Martini calls for two ounces of cognac and the juice from one lemon wedge. We experimented with proportions and found, for our taste, the recipe here features the perfect proportion of cognac and lemon juice. As for the cognac, the Hennessy VS bottling lends itself perfectly to the addition of lemon juice.

THE INTERNATIONAL COCKTAIL

Created by Dale DeGroff, beverage manager at Rainbow, New York City (see also the Añejo Highball, page 13).

Since Dale DeGroff's credentials and biography are included with his Añejo Highball recipe, it'll be more fun to discuss here Dale, the man, a very interesting character. You may have seen him on television, mixing up cocktails for the likes of Tom Snyder or on the Television Food Network (TVFN), where he appears regularly to shake, muddle, or stir up some classics, old and new. But it isn't until you have spent an hour or so at the bar with Dale that you truly fathom his passion.

Dale will eagerly show you his vast collection of cocktail books if he believes you have a true interest in the subject. Handle them carefully, now, many of his tomes are very valuable. And Dale will also croon for a crowd if there's a piano handy and the mood is right. A lover of fine cigars since well before they became de rigueur for sophisticates, Dale is a true Renaissance bartender, whose life seems to revolve around drinks and barside rituals.

The International Cocktail, a drink concocted to pay homage to the United Nations in 1995, is somewhat of a phenomenon, since it is crafted with Tennessee whiskey, a wonderfully sweet, sooty whiskey that can be very difficult to use in mixed drinks. "Since the Scots often age their whisky in sherry butts," notes Dale, "I experimented with many different sherries until I found the correct bottling: Dry Sack."

Sip an International Cocktail when you are feeling sophisticated; and if you can't quite perform the trick of twisting the orange peel and igniting the orange oils at the same time, find an equally sophisticated partner to help and make two drinks instead of one.

THE INTERNATIONAL COCKTAIL
makes 1 cocktail

2 ounces Gentleman Jack Rare Tennessee Whiskey
1 ounce Dry Sack sherry
2 dashes of Angostura bitters
1 strip of orange peel, about $1/2$ inch wide and $2^1/2$ inches long

1. Fill a mixing glass half full of ice cubes. Pour in the whiskey, sherry, and bitters and stir until well blended and chilled. Strain the drink into a chilled cocktail glass.

2. Light a match and hold it about 3 inches above the surface of the drink. Take the orange peel and carefully twist it between the thumb and forefinger of your other hand. The oils from the peel will ignite and fall to the surface of the drink. (This is a somewhat complicated procedure for one person; if need be, ask a friend to hold the match while you twist the orange peel.)

Note: It is also correct to serve this drink over ice in an old-fashioned glass.

THE JAMAICAN TEN SPEED

Created by Roger Gobler, then bartender at Café Terra Cotta, Scottsdale, Arizona.
Winner of the Smirnoff Vodka Cocktail Competition in Phoenix, 1993.

We were helping judge a cocktail competition sponsored by Smirnoff vodka. Sounds like fun, doesn't it? Yet cocktail competitions can be very deceiving at times. Before the event we looked at the drink recipes submitted by the ten finalists; their fates rested in our hands. There looked to be some decent concoctions in the running, but you never really can tell just how good a drink is until it's sliding down your throat.

A bartender from a T.G.I. Fridays by the name of Chuck "Dead Eye" Wunder was the hit of the evening. He was from the juggling school of tending bar; and dressed in a sailor's uniform, he tossed those bottles in the air as a Bette Midler tape blasted out "Boogie Woogie Bugle Boy." The crowd went wild, and the end product of Chuck's maneuver—the Boston Tea Party, an exotic takeoff on the Long Island Iced Tea—was not to be sniffed at. But little did we know what a treat we were in for when Roger Gobler, then bartender at the Café Terra Cotta, took center stage.

These days, Roger is a wine salesperson in Phoenix, but he still keeps his hand in bartending with a couple of fill-in shifts at Terra Cotta. When we contacted him, almost three years after the competition, he told us the story of his drink's creation. His first job tending bar was at a place called A Pointe in Tyme, also in Phoenix. There, he was taught how to make classic cocktails by a fellow bartender named Skip and was introduced to a regular customer by the name of Jimmy O. "Jimmy was a good drinker," says Roger. "So when I experimented with new drinks, he would help by sampling them and offering his comments."

Roger wanted to make a sweet, vodka-based drink that didn't taste too tropical; and after much experimentation (and presumably many inebriated nights for Jimmy O.), the Jamaican Ten Speed was born. The year was 1990.

The drink became so popular throughout Phoenix and was so commonly ordered in so many bars, that when Roger won the Smirnoff vodka competition, he was accused of not being the creator. But Roger did, indeed, construct the first Jamaican Ten Speed; and the drink is a superb invention. There was no doubt among the judges on that starry Arizona night that Roger's drink was the winner. It is as

memorable as an Arizona sunset. A note on Roger's entry form declares that this cocktail can be served on the rocks, at which point it becomes a Jamaican Mountain Bike. We recommend both versions.

The recipe that Roger submitted for the Smirnoff competition called for equal parts of Midori, Malibu rum, and crème de banana; but Roger says that that recipe was merely the easiest way to set the drink down on paper. After listening carefully to Roger's description of how to properly fix the drink (bartenders talk their own language, discussing amounts in terms of "counts"—how long you should keep the bottle upturned), we experimented and came up with the proportions that follow.

THE JAMAICAN TEN SPEED
makes 1 cocktail

1 ounce vodka

3/4 ounce Midori liqueur

1/4 ounce crème de banana

1/4 ounce Malibu rum

1/2 ounce half-and-half

Fill a cocktail shaker half full of ice. Add all of the ingredients and shake until creamy and well chilled. Strain into a chilled cocktail glass.

Serve at once.

JUST PEACHY
makes 1 cocktail

1½ ounces Maker's Mark bourbon
3 ounces orange juice
1½ ounces ginger ale
½ ounce peach schnapps

Fill a large goblet with ice cubes. Pour in the bourbon,
orange juice, and ginger ale; stir to blend well. Float the
peach schnapps on top. Serve at once.

JUST PEACHY

Co-created by Jimmy Conn, former director of sales for Maker's Mark bourbon, Carmen Mazurak, co-owner of Carbo's Cafe, Atlanta, and John Hadley, an executive with the Hiram Walker Company.

If you ever are lucky enough to attend the Maker's Mark's prerace brunch held on the morning of the Kentucky Derby, you will be served a Just Peachy. It will wet your whistle as you talk with others who are brimming with excitement and buzzing with tips and touts on almost every horse in the race. And though a wide variety of other drinks can be ordered, Just Peachy is most popular—perfect for daytime drinking, tart and sweet at the same time, and full of flavor all around. (The Mint Juleps come later, at Churchill Downs.) We submit that the drink is lucky, too; it spurred us to pick the Derby winner in 1996.

Jimmy Conn, the gentleman who, in 1985, created this drink with the help of Carmen Mazurak of Carbo's Cafe and John Hadley of Hiram Walker, is an old-time whiskey man. He started his career in 1954 when he worked with Pappy Van Winkle, a distillery owner who sold whiskey by the barrel in the latter years of the nineteenth century and was rumored to have sold his bourbon to moonshiners who used it to add flavor and color to their white lightning. "John, Carmen, and I were sitting around at Carbo's Cafe, a fine-dining restaurant complete with a piano bar and grand ballroom," recalls Jimmy, "and Carmen Mazurak, the owner, wanted to create a drink to personify Georgia."

Peaches, of course, were the first thing to come to mind. Together they created Just Peachy.

The staff at Carbo's goes out of its way to please its many high-powered guests; the most unusual item to originate at this restaurant must be the Coca-Cola Soufflé, created for the Coca-Cola executives from the corporate headquarters in Atlanta. Although we haven't experienced this strange-sounding dish, Carmen assures us that it works very well indeed; and if Just Peachy is anything to go by, we know that she is serious about food and drinks. "I've created a few drinks over the years," says Carmen, "but Just Peachy is the one that has remained popular for a decade and a half. It's light, refreshing, and flavorful."

THE LARK CREEK INN
TEQUILA INFUSION

Created in 1995 by chef-owner Bradley Ogden of the Lark Creek Inn, Larkspur, California.

The Lark Creek Inn Tequila Infusion was invented to celebrate the bicentennial anniversary of Jose Cuervo tequila. Elaborate dinners were held on both coasts, and award-winning chefs Bradley Ogden of the Lark Creek Inn near San Francisco, Larry Forgione of New York's An American Place restaurant, and chef-owner Carmen Ramirez Degollado of El Bajio in Mexico City teamed up to plan a festive menu for the occasion. Each course was chosen to be complemented with either straight tequila or a tequila cocktail, and Ogden's tequila infusion really caught our eye. He served it alongside his oak-fired Norwegian salmon with asparagus and spring garlic soufflé corn spoonbread. Yum.

When we first looked at the recipe for this infusion, we were somewhat mystified as to just how Chef Ogden arrived at these ingredients. But all became clear when he explained: "I needed to create a drink that could be served alongside my salmon entrée without taking anything away from the food. The pineapple was included to complement the sweet corn, and the chile also went well with the spoonbread since it, too, contains chiles. Finally, I added the tarragon, an ingredient in the broth served with the salmon. Of course, I also had to think about ingredients that would marry well to the Cuervo Traditionale, and these three choices worked perfectly."

But what made this famous chef start dabbling behind the bar? Digging into Bradley's past, we found out that he actually spent time as a bartender at a Holiday Inn and at his father's rock and roll club in Michigan. Taking the tack of creating drinks in much the same way as he cooks, Brad says that he always thinks about seasonality when preparing a drink, or a dish, and he uses fresh ingredients when their flavors are at their peak.

You should be careful on a couple of fronts when making this infusion. First, it is important to use the right tequila. The recipe was devised for Jose Cuervo Traditionale, a 100-percent agave bottling designated as a *reposado* ("rested") tequila, which means, according to Mexican governmental regulations, that the spirit has been aged in wood for a minimum of two months. The aging, albeit relatively short compared to many other spirits that sometimes stay in the wood for a decade or two, matures the tequila and gives it a complexity not found in "white" or unaged tequila. In the case of the Cuervo Traditionale, the tequila is wonderfully spicy, making it ideal for the ingredients in this particular infusion. Should you choose to use another tequila, we suggest that you find a bottling with similar qualities to the Cuervo Traditionale.

Second, you should be very careful about how long you let this mixture sit. We found that forty-eight to sixty hours works very well, but we were afraid to leave it any longer, lest the spiciness of the serrano chile start to mask the delicate tarragon.

THE LARK CREEK INN TEQUILA INFUSION
makes 12 to 14 servings

1 serrano chile pepper
1 ripe pineapple, peeled, cored, and cut into 1-inch chunks
1 large tarragon sprig
One 750-ml bottle Cuervo Traditionale tequila

1. Cut the top and tail from the chile and discard them. Halve the chile lengthwise; remove the seeds. Place the chile in a large glass container and add the pineapple and tarragon. Pour in the tequila and shake the container, if necessary, to cover all of the ingredients. Set aside in a cool, dark place for 48 to 60 hours.

2. Line a strainer or colander with a double layer of dampened cheesecloth; place it over a pitcher or large bowl. Strain the tequila; discard the pineapple, chile, and tarragon. Pour the infused tequila into a clean bottle and refrigerate or freeze for at least 12 hours.

3. Pour 2 ounces of the infusion into each small glass. Serve at once.

THE LEMON DROP

Creator unknown.

We don't know where this drink originated, but in our experience, it dates to the fall of 1991. There must be dozens of different recipes for the Lemon Drop; and the first time we saw anyone drink one (Christmas Day 1991), it was a shooter. Our dear late friend Steve Wilmot appeared at our Manhattan apartment toting a bottle of chilled Absolut Citron and a bag of lemons. "Let's do Lemon Drops!" he exclaimed.

We watched as he cut the lemons into wedges, rimmed several shot glasses with sugar, and then filled them with the liquor. "Christmas cheers," he said, as he downed the vodka, licked his lips to retrieve a few grains of sugar, and bit down on a lemon wedge.

We all mimicked him: The Lemon Drop was a sweeter, more refreshing version of the classic tequila ritual. Steve was the life and soul of that particular Christmas. Every now and then he jumped from his seat and yelled, "Let's do more Lemon Drops!"

And, oh, at least some of us did. Since then, the drink has gained in sophistication, in the process losing its ritual. We experimented with over two dozen different recipes for the Lemon Drop; some of them called for the addition of triple sec, Cointreau, and/or various other liqueurs. Indeed, one from Seattle included ginger liqueur; it was interesting, but it wasn't a Lemon Drop. Eventually, we realized that simplicity is the key to this drink. Much like the shooter we met that wonderful Christmas Day, this version calls for citrus-flavored vodka, lemon juice, and sugar.

THE LEMON DROP
makes 1 cocktail

Granulated sugar, to coat the rim of the glass

3 ounces Absolut Citron vodka

1 ounce freshly squeezed lemon juice

$^1/_2$ ounce Simple Syrup (see page 10)

1 lemon wedge

1. Moisten the outside of the rim of a cocktail glass with some of the vodka.
Sprinkle lightly but evenly with the sugar (see page 8).

2. Fill a large shaker glass two-thirds full of ice cubes. Add the vodka,
lemon juice, and simple syrup and shake until well blended and chilled.
Strain into the prepared glass; garnish with a squeeze of lemon.

LIMONCELLO

Recipe from George Germon and Johanne Killeen, chefs-co-owners of Al Forno restaurant, Providence, Rhode Island.

If you've never been to Al Forno, get there as quickly as possible. Order a wood-oven pizza, the dirty steak, and don't pass up the cookies. Be sure, too, to order a glass of Limoncello. George Germon and Johanne Killeen are culinary royalty, but don't think their passions for flavor end at the kitchen door. The bar at Al Forno offers only premium liquors and fresh-squeezed fruit juices that leave with the staff at the end of each day; none of yesterday's juices ever finds its way into a customer's glass. The bartenders are chosen just as carefully as any other staff member at this world-class restaurant. Kyle Kelly, for example, a bartender at Al Forno since around 1990 and a font of knowledge on many fronts, makes one of the best Margaritas in the country; and above all, he likes people.

In their everlasting quest for food knowledge, George and Johanne often travel to Italy; and in 1992, while staying at La Pineta, a hotel on Capri, they were introduced to the delights of Limoncello by the hotel's owner, Titina Vuotto. Titina was born to and raised in the restaurant business; both her mother and grandmother owned restaurants on Capri, and it is their recipe that she passed along to George and Johanne. Titina used to make this classic Capriote after-dinner drink with lemons from her own patio; and like most born chefs, she made it using a soupçon of this and a dash of that, so the exact quantities noted here are a result of George and Johanne's testing and experimentation.

How does one make Limoncello? Very carefully. "You must be sure to use only the yellow zest from the lemons. I recommend using a very sharp vegetable peeler or a zester," says Johanne.

The couple has also experimented with the drink by substituting vodka for the grain alcohol in this recipe. "It produces a somewhat lighter drink," says Johanne. "And we suggest that you cut down on the amount of water in the recipe, though not the sugar content, if you simply can't get grain alcohol."

Grain alcohol (95-percent/190-proof alcohol) is available only in certain states; ask your local liquor supplier if you can obtain it in your home state. And if not, ask around whenever you are out of town; it makes a world of difference to Limoncello.

LIMONCELLO

makes about 32 servings

12 medium lemons
1 liter grain alcohol
2 cups granulated sugar
2 cups water

1. Carefully pare the zest from the lemons, being careful not to take any of the white inner pith along with the zest. Place the lemon zest into a 2-quart glass container with a tight-fitting lid; reserve the pulp and juice for another use. Cover the zest with the grain alcohol and seal the container. Set aside in a cool, dark place to mellow for 1 week.

2. After 1 week, combine the sugar and water in a small saucepan. Set over moderate heat and stir frequently until the sugar dissolves and the mixture comes to a boil. Remove from the heat and let cool to room temperature.

3. When the sugar syrup has cooled, add it to the lemon zest–grain alcohol mixture. Reseal the container and set aside in a cool, dark place for 1 week longer.

4. Line a funnel with a double layer of dampened cheesecloth. Strain the Limoncello through, dividing it among clean glass bottles. Store the Limoncello in a dark place or in the freezer; it will keep indefinitely. Serve ice cold in liqueur glasses.

Note: Though Limoncello makes a superb digestif, Titina suggests that you also experiment with it in the kitchen. She adds a few drops to her zabaglione, uses it to make delightful lemon sorbets, and admits to spiking her afternoon cup of tea with a splash of it.

THE MANGO DREAM

Created in 1996 by Alfredo Ayala, chef-owner of Chayote Restaurante, San Juan, Puerto Rico.

In 1996, we traveled to Puerto Rico to explore the rum distilleries and, of course, to sample some cocktails made with Puerto Rican rum. Most of the rum consumed in the United States is made on this beautiful island by one of three producers: Bacardi, Barrilito, or Serralles. But tourists should never fear; Puerto Ricans also make sure that enough rum stays at home to keep everyone happy.

We also were served some marvelous food on this trip. Both Chayote, the restaurant where this drink was created, and Pikayo, another hot spot in San Juan, could be lifted from their native San Juan, transplanted to any major city in the United States, and there they would gain instant popularity with sophisticated foodies from far and wide. (And Pikayo, for the record, makes the best Daiquiris outside of Cuba.)

Alfredo Ayala doesn't usually turn his hand to mixing drinks—he's far too busy in the kitchen. But when the mango season arrived in 1996 (usually April through September in Puerto Rico), he decided to make good use of this local product by experimenting with mango puree and various Puerto Rican rums. Eventually, Alfredo decided to use Don Q white rum along with the El Dorado five-year-old bottling, both from the Serralles distillery. He then added fresh lime and orange juices; a touch of simple syrup; and the crowning glory: a sprig of fresh tarragon, for garnish. We had a hard time, initially, trying to figure out this tarragon; it looked like tarragon, though much larger, and was mintier than the herb we grow or buy. "It's Puerto Rican tarragon," said Alfredo. "I love what it does to this drink."

Upon arriving home, we experimented with the drink and found that good, old American-grown French tarragon works very well indeed; although we must admit that the Puerto Rican variety held a beauty all its own. Make this drink as soon as the mangoes are in season; and when you visit Puerto Rico during mango season, go to Chayote and try the original.

THE MANGO DREAM
makes 1 cocktail

1 ounce white Puerto Rican rum

1 ounce añejo Puerto Rican rum

$1/2$ ounce freshly squeezed lime juice

$1^1/_2$ ounces freshly squeezed orange juice

$1/4$ cup (2 ounces) mango puree (see note)

$1/2$ ounce Simple Syrup (see page 10; optional)

1 tarragon sprig, for garnish

Fill a large shaker glass two-thirds full of ice. Pour in both rums, both juices, the puree, and the simple syrup. Shake until blended and well chilled. Strain the drink into an ice-filled goblet; garnish with the tarragon sprig. Serve at once.

Note: To make mango puree, peel 1 ripe mango and cut the flesh away from the flat seed. Place the flesh in a blender or food processor and puree until smooth. Usually, 1 mango will produce 1 cup of puree.

MARTINI THYME

Created by Ted and Linda Fondulas owners of Hemingway's restaurant in Killington, Vermont (see also the Burnt Orange Kir, page 25).

"*We find it important* to keep our customers interested in our food—and in our drinks," says Linda Fondulas. "After all, it's our job to offer flavors, and flavor in a glass is just as important as that on a plate."

More about Hemingway's and the Fondulas couple accompanies the recipe for the Burnt Orange Kir, but let it be said here that their Martini Thyme is one of the few Martini variations we have chosen to include in this book. As with most drinks that stand a chance of attaining classic status, it is the drink's simplicity that makes it stand above the crowd.

Martini Thyme is a simple mixture of London dry gin and Chartreuse, but each of these spirits is incredibly complex in and of itself. Chartreuse, a liqueur made by Carthusian monks since 1605, is said to include 130 different ingredients in its secret recipe. Most distillers of London dry gin are equally evasive in naming their ingredients; but gin, too, contains a complex blend of herbs and spices, and some recipes are said to date back to the mid-eighteenth century. However, it's the sprig of thyme that adds the oomph to this drink; its aroma mingles beautifully at the back of your throat with the flavors of the gin and Chartreuse. Just give it a try.

MARTINI THYME
makes 1 cocktail

3 ounces gin

3/4 ounce Chartreuse
(green or yellow, each makes a different, but equally wonderful drink)

1 thyme sprig, for garnish

Fill a mixing glass two-thirds full of ice cubes. Add the gin and Chartreuse and stir until well chilled. Strain into a chilled cocktail glass; garnish with the thyme sprig. Serve at once.

THE METROPOLITAN
makes 1 cocktail

2 ounces Absolut Kurant vodka

1/2 ounce lime juice cordial,
such as Rose's or Angostura lime juice

1/2 ounce freshly squeezed lime juice

1 ounce cranberry juice

1 lime wedge, for garnish

Fill a large shaker glass two-thirds full of ice cubes. Add the
vodka, lime cordial, lime juice, and cranberry juice. Shake
until well blended and chilled. Strain into a chilled cocktail
glass; garnish with the lime wedge.

THE METROPOLITAN

Created in 1993 by Chuck Coggins, bartender at Marion's Continental Restaurant & Lounge, New York City.

Down on New York's Bowery lives a funky bar by the name of Marion's Continental Restaurant & Lounge. When it opened its doors in 1950, Marion's was owned by fashion model Marion Nagy, who as a member of communist Hungary's official swimming team had sought refuge in the West while representing her country at the Paris Peace Games after World War II. After modeling professionally in Paris, Marion set sail for the land of the free and became part of the bohemian downtown scene, while modeling in New York City. She had a knack for bringing interesting people together for nights out in the Big Apple; and when a fashionable friend suggested she open a restaurant, she went straight out and did just that. Marion's flourished until she retired in 1973.

Seventeen years later, Marion's was restored to its former 1950s splendor and reopened in July 1990. The magic had lingered. Walk into Marion's on any night of the week and you will find the new bohemian downtown crowd sitting at the bar. There are gays, there are straights, and there are in-betweens. It's a funky crowd, but everyone—from Wall Street bankers to New Age poets—feels comfortable at Marion's. If your timing is good, you are likely to see Chuck Coggins, bartender extraordinaire, behind the mahogany.

Chuck is an unassuming type. When we first asked him about how he had created the masterpiece cocktail he named the Metropolitan, his reply was typical. "It's no big deal. Absolut Kurant was new on the market so I poured some into the cocktail shaker, added some extra ingredients, and called it the Metropolitan."

But this drink has enjoyed widespread success; it's a modern-day classic that appears on cocktail menus across the country. But as with every true classic, each bartender puts his or her own twist on the drink. This is Chuck's original recipe.

MEZCAL MARGARITA
makes 1 cocktail

1 ounce Encantado mezcal

$^1/_3$ ounce brandy or cognac

$1^1/_3$ ounces freshly squeezed lime juice

$^2/_3$ ounce Simple Syrup (see page 10)

2 to 3 dashes of Peychaud bitters

1 lime wheel, for garnish

Fill a large shaker glass half full of ice cubes.
Pour in the mezcal, brandy, lime juice, simple syrup,
and bitters. Shake until well blended and chilled.
Strain into a chilled Margarita glass; float the
lime wheel on top. Serve at once.

MEZCAL MARGARITA

Created by Rick Bayless, chef-owner of Topolobampo and Frontera Grill, Chicago.

Though you might not have tasted mezcal, we bet you've heard about it: It's what many people refer to as "that Mexican liquor that has the dead worm in the bottle." And, no, it's not tequila, though the two products share their main ingredient: agave. Until recently, mezcal was mezcal; no single brand had more clout than others. It seemed that all mezcals were created alike: rough on the palate and throat, but easy to toss back as a shooter. No doubt you—or someone you know—can recount your first visit to Nogales or Tijuana or another border town, and that's where mezcal will ring a bell. Who could resist bringing back a bottle of liquor with a worm?

Then, in 1995, Encantado mezcal was introduced. Thank heaven, there is no worm in this amazingly fine, hand-crafted bottling made in Oaxaca. And when celebrated chef Rick Bayless tasted the Encantado, he created his Mezcal Margarita from this new, more refined liquor.

Encantado mezcal is made from a few different varieties of agave, including the blue agave used to produce tequila. The result is a refined, smoky spirit with multilayered flavors that pepper the tongue and delight the throat. But this is a liquor that's hard to mix successfully with other ingredients; like whiskey, Encantado just isn't the marrying kind. Nevertheless, Rick Bayless paved the way: "I experimented with mezcal-based drinks for over a year before I hit on this particular recipe. Most of the ingredients I married to this spirit simply melted into the background while the smokiness of the mezcal overpowered the whole drink. But then I added Peychaud bitters to my mezcal recipes; the drinks were just so much more adult. Bitters add an unparalleled complexity to many drinks."

We wholeheartedly agree—don't miss this one. Here's a recipe that's been adapted from Rick's original.

THE MINNESOTA MANHATTAN
makes 1 cocktail

3 ounces Stolichnaya Okhotnichya vodka
1 ounce sweet vermouth
2 dashes of Angostura bitters
$^1/_2$ ounce water
1 dried cherry, for garnish

Fill a mixing glass two-thirds full of ice. Add the vodka, vermouth, bitters, and water. Stir until well chilled. Strain the drink into a chilled cocktail glass; garnish with the cherry. Serve at once.

THE MINNESOTA MANHATTAN

Created in 1992 by Jacqui Smith, co-owner with Jay Savulich
of the Grange Hall, New York City.

Why on earth, we wondered, is this drink called the Minnesota Manhattan? It's made from flavored Russian vodka, Italian vermouth, and bitters from Trinidad. "The Grange Hall has a Midwestern profile," says creator Jacqui Smith, "and Minnesota went well with Manhattan."

But don't let Jacqui's flip attitude about the name fool you—she's a dedicated connoisseur of cocktails.

During her childhood as a Navy brat, Jacqui's father often moonlighted as a bartender; and she sometimes would visit him to watch him make his various classic potions. At age eighteen she started waiting tables in Woodstock, New York; and shortly found herself in the Big Apple, working at several restaurants and occasionally booking acts for the home of jazz fusion, Seventh Avenue South.

Gulf Coast, an immensely successful restaurant in New York, was one of the first places that Jacqui helped open; and by that time, she had one of those wonderful jobs that required her to tend bar, wait tables, and help manage the joint. While working there she, and fellow worker Jay Savulich, started work on the Midwestern theme that would result in the 1992 opening of Grange Hall. "But the bar was always my first love," says Jacqui, "even when I couldn't actually tend bar, I could always find time to create new drinks."

And the cocktail menu at the Grange Hall is, indeed, impressive.

The Minnesota Manhattan was created because Jacqui doesn't like the effect of whiskey on her system; and she was, well, sort of jealous of her many friends who drank Manhattans. When Jacqui first tried Okhotnichya vodka she realized that the spirit had enough body and flavor to be married to sweet vermouth, but she wouldn't reap a whiskey hangover by drinking it. This drink is marvelously complex; just think about the ingredients: Vermouth is flavored with many botanicals; this particular vodka contains ginger, cloves, anise, and many other flavorings; and Angostura bitters is just about as complex as anything you can imagine. Sometimes marrying three such convoluted liquids just doesn't work; but in this case, it results in a spicy nectar fit for drinking from coast to coast.

NIKOS AT NITE
makes 2 cocktails

1/2 ounce Baileys Irish Cream
1/2 ounce Frangelico
1/2 ounce Marie Brizard Chocolat Royal
1/4 ounce white crème de menthe

Fill a shaker glass half full of ice cubes. Add all of the ingredients and shake until well blended and chilled. Strain into two 2-ounce liqueur glasses. Serve ice cold.

NIKOS AT NITE

Created in 1996 by Nick Hydos, manager-bartender at Painter's Tavern,
Cornwall-on-Hudson, New York.

In 1995 we decided to leave the Big Apple and look for a more peaceful environment where we could mix drinks to the sounds of birds and crickets rather than blaring sirens. But where to go? After more than twenty years in a city that we both truly love, it was hard to think of straying too far. Cornwall-on-Hudson was perfect. The idyllic village is just over fifty miles from Manhattan; and it sports a diverse, sophisticated community and a great restaurant: Painter's Tavern. Painter's serves wonderful, casual food prepared by chef Donna Hammond and employs a friendly staff that remembers your face after just one visit. This restaurant is the local that everyone dreams of having at the corner of their street—it was one of the reasons that we never looked at another town during our search for a new home.

Nick has been a professional bartender for just the six years since he retired from a career in the airline catering business. "It was a very stressful job," says Nick. "When I retired, I would pop into Painter's Tavern to visit my daughter Kathy who works there still. On a couple of occasions I jumped in to help out when the bar got crowded, and I ended up being offered a full-time manager-bartender position."

Nick's other daughter, Irene, also works at Painter's these days; and sometimes you can visit Painter's and see the whole Hydos clan—some working, some out for dinner. Nick loves the life behind the bar, and when he retires he intends to settle in Greece, where he dreams of tending bar at a more leisurely pace.

Nikos at Nite makes a delightful shooter, but it's also pleasing for sipping after dinner or in lieu of dessert. We believe that the secret of this drink's appeal lies in the small proportion of crème de menthe; the wonderful mix of Baileys, Frangelico, and Marie Brizard Chocolat Royal is startlingly heightened by the delicate touch of mint that tingles at the back of your throat.

THE OATMEAL COOKIE
makes 1 cocktail

1 ounce Baileys Irish Cream
1 ounce Jägermeister
1 ounce butterscotch schnapps
$1/2$ ounce cinnamon schnapps
Dark and golden raisins and ground cinnamon, for garnish

Fill a large shaker glass two-thirds full of ice cubes. Pour in the Baileys, Jägermeister, and both flavors of schnapps. Shake until well blended and chilled. Strain into an ice-filled goblet or tumbler. Thread the raisins on a skewer and serve as a swizzle stick garnish; lightly sprinkle with cinnamon.

THE OATMEAL COOKIE

Creator unknown.

We couldn't resist this drink because it's a sign of the times. A number of cocktails have appeared over the past few years that are likened to food products: There's a drink called the Girl Scout Cookie and another named Special K; not to mention drinks that are supposed to taste like jelly beans, Dr. Pepper, and a peach melba ice cream sundae. Our favorite creation in this genre, however, is the Oatmeal Cookie.

We discovered this drink on the Internet, where we saw many variations on the recipe and experimented with all of them. Our favorite combination of ingredients included butterscotch schnapps, Baileys Irish Cream, cinnamon schnapps, and Jägermeister; but the recipes that used this particular combination indicated that the ingredients should be added in equal proportions. Not so according to our palates; we fussed and we blustered until we had perfected the formula to deserve its name.

And unbelievable as it may seem, the key ingredient to the most toothsome Oatmeal Cookie is Jägermeister, a German cordial that has soared in popularity in recent years. Walk into any college bar, and you are bound to catch young drinkers downing ice-cold shots of this complex formula. Indeed, it's so popular at some spots that it's dispensed from a tap, like beer, rather than poured by hand from the bottle. What we think is most interesting, however, is the flavor of Jägermeister, the product of fifty-six herbs, fruits, and spices: It's downright medicinal. How can this stuff make the difference in this cocktail? And yet, it does.

Jägermeister has been available in Europe since 1935. When used as a digestif—straight from the freezer after a large dinner—it shocks you right out of that time-to-retire-to-a-plush-armchair mood, gets conversation flowing again, and simultaneously has a wonderful calming affect on your overfull tummy. In the Oatmeal Cookie, it is Jägermeister that brings all the other ingredients together in harmony.

THE PACIFIC RIM
makes 1 cocktail

3 ounces vodka

$1/2$ ounce Original Canton Delicate Ginger Liqueur

1 strip of crystallized ginger, for garnish

Fill a large mixing glass two-thirds full of ice cubes. Add the
vodka and liqueur; stir until well blended and chilled.
Strain into a chilled cocktail glass; garnish with the
crystallized ginger. Serve at once.

GIN VARIATION

2 ounces London dry gin

1 ounce Original Canton Delicate Ginger Liqueur

1 strip of crystallized ginger

Follow the directions for the original Pacific Rim.

THE PACIFIC RIM

Created in 1993 by Ginger DiLello, head bartender at Philadelphia Fish and Company, Philadelphia.

Before it became known as the Pacific Rim (an appropriate name bestowed on the drink by marketers), Ginger DiLello, head bartender and resident artist at Philadelphia Fish and Company, created the Ginger Martini: a glorious five-to-one mix of Stolichnaya vodka and Original Canton Delicate Ginger Liqueur. She garnished the drink with a slice of starfruit (or whatever exotic fruit was available) and served it to her regular customers who were familiar with her expertise behind the bar. "I try to make new drinks every Friday," says Ginger (whose hair color "usually" matches her name). "My regulars will sidle up to the bar and order whatever it is I've just created. The Ginger Martini was something I concocted when Canton first hit the marketplace. It has become very popular at Philadelphia Fish and Company."

Ginger certainly is creative when it comes to mixing drinks; she once made a Hockey Puck, which was served in black ashtrays, and the whole crowd at the bar tried them out. Her resident artist status comes from a blackboard in the restaurant that is devoted to whatever chalk drawings she cares to execute. When we spoke to her, she had just completed a rendition of one of Cézanne's *Large Bathers* series—no wacky cartoon characters allowed.

Ginger's original recipe for the Pacific Rim is a divine creation; but we have also experimented with the drink using London dry gin instead of vodka, and find that the gin version is best made with two parts gin to one part Canton. We add a strip of crystallized ginger to either drink; it's a wonderful tidbit to nibble as you sip this very sophisticated cocktail.

PAINTER'S PUNCH
makes 1 cocktail

1 ounce Chambord
1 ounce Southern Comfort
1 ounce pineapple juice
1 ounce cranberry juice
1 maraschino cherry, for garnish

Fill a double old-fashioned glass with ice. Add the
Chambord, Southern Comfort, and both juices. Stir to
blend; garnish with the maraschino cherry. Serve at once.

PAINTER'S PUNCH

Created in 1995 by Steve Scalzo, bartender at Painter's Tavern,
Cornwall-on-Hudson, New York.

Steve Scalzo grew up in Utica, New York, with Larry Wolhandler and Sal Buttiglieri, owners of Painter's Tavern in our new hometown. When Steve stopped by for a visit in 1985, little did he know that Painter's Tavern would figure in his future. Typical of an old friend with a can-do attitude, Steve got roped into helping out around the bar-restaurant; and he was hooked. He soon moved to Cornwall. Originally a piano tuner and rock and roll keyboard player with a degree in music from Oswego State University, Steve has tuned pianos for the likes of Ray Charles, Ella Fitzgerald, Fats Domino, Tony Bennett, and Ozzie Osborne as well as spending a decade on the road with rock and roll bands such as Dyno-Soar. But for the past ten years, while tuning pianos during the day, Steve has had a regular gig behind the bar at Painter's, where his deft finger action shakes, muddles, and stirs to a tune that only he can hear. The resultant drinks, however, are applauded by all.

Painter's Punch is a somewhat sweetish drink, but the cranberry juice adds just the right amount of tartness to give it a sophisticated quality that sets it apart from most drinks of this genre. Steve created it in 1995 as both a shooter and an on-the-rocks drink, and it has been flying over the bar in copious quantities ever since. We recommend that you sip a Painter's Punch on the deck or by the pool while you watch the sun go down over the mighty Hudson.

PARIS IS BURNING

makes 1 cocktail

2 ounces cognac
1/2 ounce Chambord
1 lemon twist

To heat in a microwave oven: Pour the cognac and Chambord into a large snifter. Place the glass in a microwave oven and warm on high power for 20 seconds. Garnish with the lemon twist.

To heat on stovetop: Combine the cognac and Chambord in a nonreactive small saucepan. Place over low heat and warm until slightly warmer than body temperature, 30 to 60 seconds. Watch carefully to ensure that the alcohol doesn't ignite. Pour into a snifter and serve at once.

PARIS IS BURNING

Creator unknown.

In the late 1980's Kevin O'Brien, an executive at "America's Oldest Cordial Producers," Chas. Jacquin et Cie, Inc., was dining with friends at Salty's on Alki, a Seattle restaurant. The night was cool and rainy—a somewhat frequent occurrence in that particular neck of the woods—and after dinner, Kevin ordered one of his company's products, Chambord. The bartender, whom we have been unable to track down, asked if he could mix him one of his creations: Chambord and brandy heated by the steam from the cappuccino machine. Kevin complied; and after tasting the cocktail, the marketing wheels in his head began to turn.

Some time later, while dining with Norton Cooper, chairman of the board of Chambord et Cie, Kevin suggested that they market the drink. The pair played around with proportions, settling on a fifty-fifty mix, and came up with the name "Is Paris Burning?" to stress the French ingredients. The recipe was published in a promotional brochure for Chambord, a dark, rich liqueur made from black raspberries, other fruits, herbs, and honey.

By 1996, the name and the proportions of the drink had altered somewhat. It is now known as Paris Is Burning, probably because of the low-budget but popular film of the same name; and bartenders across the country are making the drink with more cognac than Chambord. One of the beauties of Paris Is Burning is that you can alter the proportions to suit everyone's taste: Add more Chambord for a sweeter potion or less for a drier, somewhat more sophisticated after-dinner drink.

We experimented with Paris Is Burning on many a cold night during the long winter of 1995–1996 and came up with the proportions listed here. We also added the twist of lemon that gives the drink its wonderfully sharp nose.

PASSIONNÉ

Created in 1992 by Andreas Noeth, head bartender at the Mark Hotel, New York City.

*W*hen *Andreas Noeth* tells you that tending bar is in his blood, you'd better believe him. His grandfather ran a small guest house in Germany that had been in the family for over two hundred years, his father has worked in the restaurant business his entire working life, and his great-uncle made a pretty penny during Prohibition when he ran a speakeasy in the Wall Street area of Manhattan. Following in his family's footsteps, Andreas tended bar for a few years in Queens, New York, until in 1991, he started work as a bartender at the prestigious Mark Hotel in Manhattan.

"Food and beverage director Jean-Luc Deguines taught me how to be a true professional behind the bar. I owe an awful lot to Jean-Luc," says Andreas. "In a hotel bar a bartender gets the chance to refine his or her art. The customers are sophisticated—often world travelers—and they aren't afraid to try something new."

Andreas's cocktail, the Passionné, is a superb example of his art, and the way he created it gives insight into the mind of a professional bartender. "Initially, I made the drink with passion fruit and raspberry purees," Andreas recalls. "But when I stirred them together with the champagne, the wine lost much of its effervescence. Then I found Alizé Passion brandy, which made a perfect substitute for the passion fruit, and Chambord was a natural choice to use in place of the raspberries. Truth is, whenever I create a new drink, it normally takes me a few months to get the ingredients and the proportions to the point where I'm happy with the results."

Passionné is a huge hit at the Mark Hotel, and we think it will be a hit at your house, too.

PASSIONNÉ
makes 1 cocktail

1 1/2 ounces Alizé Passion brandy

1/2 ounce Chambord

6 ounces champagne

4 ounces freshly squeezed orange juice

10 raspberries

Fill a large goblet with ice cubes. Pour in the brandy, Chambord, champagne, and orange juice. Stir to blend well. Add the raspberries and stir again.
Serve at once.

THE PINK LEMONADE
makes 1 cocktail

Granulated sugar, to coat the rim of the glass

$2^{1}/_{2}$ ounces Bacardi Limón

1 ounce Cointreau

$^{1}/_{2}$ ounce freshly squeezed lemon juice

$^{1}/_{2}$ ounce cranberry juice

$^{1}/_{2}$ lemon slice, for garnish

1. Moisten the rim of a cocktail glass with some of the Bacardi Limón; sprinkle lightly but evenly with the sugar (see page 8).

2. Fill a large shaker glass two-thirds full of ice cubes. Add the Bacardi Limón, Cointreau, lemon juice, and cranberry juice; shake until well blended and chilled. Strain into the prepared glass; garnish with the lemon slice. Serve at once.

THE PINK LEMONADE

Created by Bryna O'Shea, bartender at Palomino Euro Bistro, San Francisco.

Bryna O'Shea is a New Yorker's New Yorker and a bartender's bartender. Her first stint behind the stick was in 1970 at McDonnell's Cafe in Great Neck, Long Island; and if you ever visit Bryna at her present location, ask her to tell you some of her tales of the old days at McDonnell's—it sounds like quite a joint. From there, in the grand tradition of tending bar, Bryna moved around from bar to bar, on Long Island and then on to New York City, where she ended up at El Rio Grande, a popular Tex-Mex restaurant with a bar that's always several drinkers deep.

In 1990, Bryna moved to San Francisco where, once again, she moved around, working at Oritalia in Ghirardelli Square and Splendido, an immensely popular Mediterranean restaurant owned by the Kimpton Group. Why did Bryna flit around so much? The fact is, many true professionals do the exact same thing; sometimes they get bored with one crowd of customers and go looking for a bar with a clientele better suited to their style, sometimes a new manager is hired who doesn't give the old staff the same leeway as the previous one, and in some instances they just *feel* that it's time for a change. The advantage of working so many restaurants is that at each one the bartender learns something new.

Bryna finally found her home in 1993 at Palomino Euro Bistro, where she is known for making the best Cosmopolitan cocktail in Fog City. "Pink Lemonade is based on the Cosmopolitan," says Bryna. "Bacardi Limón was introduced in 1994, and I played around with it for a while until I devised this particular drink."

Though the Pink Lemonade was created for summertime consumption, we suggest you serve it any time you want a refreshing bracer or a tart apéritif.

THE RIALTO BIANCO

Created in 1995 by Esti Benson, manager of the Rialto Restaurant in the Charles Hotel, Cambridge, Massachusetts.

Esti Benson took a travel break from work between her job at the much-acclaimed Michela's restaurant in Cambridge and her new one, as manager of what would be the much-acclaimed Rialto, working alongside general manager-partner Christopher Myers and chef-partner Jody Adams. The Jody-Christopher dynamic duo offered a creative place for such as Esti, and she took the opportunity to travel to Europe to become better versed in the regional foods and drinks—mainly Spanish, French, and Italian—that would be offered.

"I tended bar at Michela's," says Esti, "and it was there that I learned to experiment with cocktails. But although I'm no longer behind the bar, I still love to conceptualize new drinks."

Time spent in Italy provided the inspiration she needed to create the Rialto Bianco. Picture her there, sitting over a salad that contained lots of basil. She remembers, "I was sipping a glass of Cinzano Bianco alongside the salad, and I kept noticing how well the flavors went together."

On returning to Massachusetts, Esti set about finding the correct proportions to make a basil-flavored vermouth cocktail.

"We first made the drink using only the Bianco vermouth," says Esti, "but it was a little too sweet. Eventually I tried adding some dry vermouth to the infused Bianco. Then we just added a splash of club soda and a basil leaf for garnish, and the Rialto Bianco was born."

This drink is astonishingly refreshing. We suggest you sip it when the sun is beating down on your fevered brow and you need to forget about the world for a while. Christopher, a born wag, suggests that the Rialto Bianco goes well with chicken, pasta, Saturday afternoons, life, romance, and Jell-O wrestling. We agree with five of his notions.

THE RIALTO BIANCO
makes 1 cocktail

$1^1/_2$ ounces Basil-Infused Bianco Vermouth (recipe below)

$1^1/_2$ ounces Cinzano dry vermouth

Splash of club soda

1 basil leaf, for garnish

Fill a shaker glass two-thirds full of ice cubes. Add both vermouths and shake until well blended and chilled. Fill a double old-fashioned glass or wineglass with ice cubes. Strain the vermouth mixture into the glass; add a splash of soda. Garnish with the basil leaf and serve at once.

BASIL-INFUSED BIANCO VERMOUTH
makes about 24 ounces

Be sure to prepare this the day before you plan to use it.
It's so good, you'll want to keep some in the refrigerator for any number of uses.

One 750-ml bottle Cinzano Bianco

About 15 large basil leaves, washed, dried, and stemmed

1. Pour the vermouth into a glass container with a tight-fitting lid and add the basil leaves. Stir briefly, close the container, and set aside overnight.

2. Line a funnel with a double layer of dampened cheesecloth. Pour the infused vermouth through it into a clean bottle or pitcher. Discard the basil leaves. Pour the infusion back into its bottle. Store in the refrigerator for up to 6 months.

THE RUMBO JAM

Created by Katy Keck, co-owner of the New World Grill in Manhattan and owner of Savoir Faire Foods, a catering company.

Katy Keck is a colorful character, a genius at marrying intricate flavors, and a dear friend. She started her working career on Wall Street where she was involved with the treasury and marketing departments of some high-powered banks and, as a sideline, took a catering class where her talents in the kitchen were first recognized. Encouraged by her tutor, Katy started to enter recipe competitions, and in 1986 she won a two-month chef's apprenticeship in France. After extending her stay by working in Parisian restaurants for more than a year, Katy returned to New York City and opened Savoir Faire Foods, a catering company that specializes in recipe development and food styling.

You've all seen food Katy has prepared. She firmly established herself in New York food circles by performing food-styling magic for television shows, such as *Live with Regis and Kathie Lee*, *Late Night with David Letterman*, *Today*, and *CBS This Morning*. Then in 1993 Katy, with partner Richard Barber, opened the New World Grill. There you will find some of Katy's most inspired flavor combinations. She describes the menu as Continental-American with Asian influences, and the same could be said of her drink the Rumbo Jam.

The drink was initially a frozen concoction, created as a substitute potion for the restaurant's frozen Margarita machine. However, after Katy discovered that customers loved Rumbo Jams but were still demanding frozen Margaritas, it became a mixed drink.

We weren't surprised to find some ginger juice in the Rumbo Jam; Katy tends to be a fiend for ginger. Ideally, you should feed fresh ginger into a juicer to get every last drop of juice out of the root, but if you don't have a juicer, simply grate the ginger onto a square of dampened cheesecloth (peel and all—it doesn't matter), gather the four corners together to contain the grated root, and squeeze, *hard*, over a glass. A one-inch piece of ginger should render enough juice for half a dozen Rumbo Jams. The other alternative, should you find some in an Asian food store, is canned (or jarred) sweet red ginger, which should be pureed before you add it to the drink. Whatever you do, however, don't leave out the ginger juice; it's integral to this drink.

Why Rumbo Jam? Katy used to offer a nonalcoholic drink at the New World Grill, made without rum or lime juice, known as a Juice Jamboree. Add the rum and you have a rum jamboree, and after mixing up the letters and throwing a few of them away, you are left with the Rumbo Jam.

The Rumbo Jam is a summertime drink with adult flavors—not one of those extra-sweet concoctions that are often served by the pool at resort hotels. This drink has a kick, it has a thirst-quenching dryness, and it has an I-want-more-ish quality that can make it a tad dangerous should you be in the mood for glugging your drink rather than sipping it. Remember, there's a full three ounces of rum in a Rumbo Jam.

THE RUMBO JAM
makes 1 cocktail

3 ounces light rum

2 ounces pineapple juice

1 1/2 ounces cranberry juice

1/2 ounce freshly squeezed lime juice

1 teaspoon fresh ginger juice

Fill a large shaker two-thirds full of ice cubes. Add all of the ingredients and shake until well blended and chilled. Fill a large glass with fresh ice cubes. Strain the drink over the ice and serve at once.

SAUZA-ROX

Created by Jim Hewes, bartender at the Round Robin Bar at the
Willard Intercontinental Hotel, Washington, D.C.

We first spotted Jim Hewes on television in 1994 when he was interviewed on CNBC by Tom Snyder. With him were other notables: Dale DeGroff of New York's Rainbow Room and Pepe the bartender at the now-closed Chasen's of Hollywood. We must praise Snyder for having the guts to talk about hard liquor and cocktails on national television, and we thank him for introducing these three master bartenders to the country at large.

Jim Hewes is a born bartender. At Denison University in Granville, Ohio, where he majored in history and education, Jim devised a bartending course for college credits. And when he graduated from college, his first job was as beverage manager at the Buxton Inn in Granville, Ohio's oldest inn in continuous business and in its original building. Eventually, after working for a decade in restaurant management, Jim went back to his first love: tending bar. And he found his home at the Round Robin Bar at the Willard Intercontinental Hotel in Washington, D.C. Since the hotel was steeped in history, Jim managed to use his education while shaking and stirring for the movers and shakers in the nation's capital.

Along with creating many drinks of his own, Jim is also a master of reviving old classic cocktails, such as the Clover Club, and loves to use some old-time methods of fixing drinks. Famed nineteenth-century bartender and author of *How to Mix Drinks*, Professor Jerry Thomas was fond of combining ingredients by pouring them back and forth between two large glasses. Jim picked up that cue and reintroduced this method of mixing when he featured an array of fizzes on the Round Robin's cocktail menu.

The Sauza-Rox is Jim's homage to the absinthe cocktails of New Orleans, birthplace of the classic Sazerac cocktail, a drink reportedly created by nineteenth-century New Orleans bartender Leon Lamothe. But in addition to making the Sauza-Rox in a glass coated in absinthe substitute and adding Peychaud bitters (products without which the Sazerac is simply not a Sazerac), Jim has incorporated a method of adding just the right amount of sugar to this drink, which harks back to the old absinthe drinkers of Paris and New Orleans. Absinthe has been illegal in most countries since around 1914, but when Van Gogh and Toulouse-Lautrec, both lovers of what was then known as the Green Fairy, prepared their potions, they did so by pouring water over a sugar cube that sat atop an absinthe spoon that rested on the glass. Absinthe spoons are perforated, trowel-shaped, flat spoons created exclusively for this very purpose (see the photo), and although they are hard to find, if you are ever in France, you should scour antique stores for these valuable objects.

Of course, you don't need a true absinthe spoon to create the Sauza-Rox, a tea strainer will suffice; or you can follow Jim's method of adding a sugar cube to the shaker without allowing the cube to dissolve completely before you strain the drink into the glass. This way, the drink contains just the right amount of sugar. Jim's original drink called for Sauza Conmemorativo tequila, and that bottling is excellent in his drink. Feel free, however, to use any tequila you fancy, although we do suggest an añejo (aged) bottling.

SAUZA-ROX
makes 1 cocktail

¹/₂ ounce absinthe substitute (Herbsaint, Pernod, or Ricard)

Crushed ice

2 ounces Sauza Conmemorativo tequila

2 ounces freshly squeezed orange juice

2 dashes of Peychaud bitters

1 sugar cube

1. Pour the absinthe substitute into a goblet or wineglass, swirl it around to coat the inside of the glass, and pour out any excess. Fill the glass with crushed ice.

2. Fill a large shaker glass two-thirds full of ice cubes. Pour in the tequila, orange juice, and bitters; add the sugar cube. Shake until the sugar cube dissolves somewhat and the liquids are well mixed. Strain the drink into the prepared glass of crushed ice. Serve at once.

THE SEELBACH COCKTAIL

Created in 1917 by an unknown bartender at Louisville's Seelbach Hotel
and rediscovered in 1995.

The Seelbach, Louisville's grand hotel, opened in 1905 and was later immortalized by F. Scott Fitzgerald in *The Great Gatsby.* It's our favorite haunt in downtown Louisville, Kentucky. The Old Seelbach Bar feels like an elegant, early-twentieth-century saloon—a bar built on the backs of race horses and the staves of charred oak whiskey barrels—and is *the* meeting place in the city. If you want to know what's going on in Louisville, the Old Seelbach is the place to be.

The tale behind the Seelbach Cocktail is a somewhat complicated affair. This is the first time that the recipe has ever been seen in print; and to our knowledge, no more than four people have known the ingredients until now. The drink was created in 1917 when, according to legend, a bartender popped open a bottle of champagne that immediately started to shoot its contents into the air. The bartender, in an attempt to contain the spill, grabbed a customer's Manhattan cocktail to catch the bubbly. After making a fresh drink for the customer, the bartender sipped on his mistake, made a few refinements, and the Seelbach Cocktail was born. The recipe, however, was lost during the great American drought known as Prohibition.

In 1995, Adam Seger became the director of restaurants at the hotel, and this able young man unearthed the recipe. Many people would have passed it by, but not Adam; he immediately reintroduced the drink at the hotel, mixing the triple sec and bitters in a private room, issuing his secret formula to the barstaff, and promoting the drink that once was lost but now was found. After tasting this delightful potion, we just had to find out exactly what was in Adam's secret mix.

"Sorry, it's a secret," we were told.

But in time, Adam had a change of heart. A few weeks later he called, "If I were to tell you the ingredients, would you agree to keep them to yourselves until publication of the book?" he asked.

"Of course," we replied, "what do you have in mind?"

"I'm going to run a contest wherein guests can try to figure out exactly what's in the drink, and we will reward the person who comes closest just before your book hits the market."

It sounded like a good excuse for a party, and so, naturally, we agreed.

Here, then, is the recipe for the Seelbach Cocktail. The Seelbach makes theirs using Korbel Brut sparkling wine and Old Forester bourbon, but we think any brut champagne or sparkling wine will do. We do, though, recommend that you stick with the Old Forester or another old-fashioned, pre-Prohibition bourbon whiskey that's full of guts and flavor.

THE SEELBACH COCKTAIL

makes 1 cocktail

1 ounce Old Forester bourbon

1/2 ounce triple sec

7 dashes of Angostura bitters

7 dashes of Peychaud bitters

5 ounces chilled Korbel Brut

1 orange twist, for garnish

Combine the bourbon, triple sec, and both bitters in a champagne flute;
stir briefly, just to blend. Pour in the champagne. Twist the orange peel and
rub the exterior of it around the rim of the flute; drop the twist into the cocktail.
Serve at once.

THE SFUZZI SFIZZ

Created in 1992 by Raul Adorno, then bartender at Sfuzzi restaurant, New York City.

Raul Adorno is a professional bartender, and in the manner of many masters of the craft, he started out as a bar-back. Bar-backs cut fruit; fetch ice; replace the empty beer, wine, and liquor bottles; and generally make the bartender's life a little easier. For people who want to tend bar for a living, this job is a great way to get a foot in the door at a fine restaurant and a grand opportunity to learn by watching experts. In Raul's case, he worked at the Hyatt in New York for about a year before he was promoted to a bartending position.

Raul left Hyatt in 1987; took a year off to hang out in California; and returned to New York to work at Aquavit, a highly acclaimed Scandinavian restaurant, before he found his job at Sfuzzi, a hip Italian restaurant that serves innovative food and offers a great selection of drinks. Sfuzzi, and Raul, worked closely with Finlandia vodka to create many vodka infusions, and indeed, the concept of infusing vodka was popularized by Finlandia when they introduced their infusion program in 1990. They began by offering recipes and special decanters to restaurants nationwide and then encouraged bartenders to create their own concoctions. Most such promotions seem to fizzle out after six to twelve months, but this particular plan has gone from strength to strength and continues to grow.

Raul is also moving from strength to strength. Although in 1996 he returned to Sfuzzi for a while to teach the bar manager and bartenders how to infuse vodkas successfully, he currently tends bar at Morton's of Chicago in Manhattan's Wall Street area. Will he always tend bar? "I think so," says Raul. "I was an anthropology major in college and being with people while exploring different cultures is my first love. Where better to meet interesting people than from behind the bar?"

In our opinion, the crowning glory of Raul's infusions is the Sfuzzi Sfizz. The sweet fruit flavors of the strawberries and blood orange marry with the tart lemon juice in the glass; and when topped with club soda, this summertime drink is at once complex and refreshing. You may want to experiment with the amount of simple syrup you add to the Sfuzzi Sfizz, but the ratio given here is our favorite.

THE SFUZZI SFIZZ
makes 1 cocktail

2 ounces Sfuzzi Sfizz Infused Vodka (recipe below)

$^1/_2$ ounce Simple Syrup (see page 10)

1 ounce freshly squeezed lemon juice

6 ounces club soda

1 blood orange slice, for garnish

Fill a large, tall glass two-thirds full of ice cubes. Add the infused vodka, simple syrup, and lemon juice; top with the club soda. Stir briefly with a long straw or chopstick. Garnish with the blood orange slice.

THE SFUZZI SFIZZ INFUSED VODKA
makes about 24 ounces

One 750-ml bottle vodka

2 pints fresh strawberries, hulled

1 blood orange, peeled and sliced

1. Pour the vodka into a very large, wide-mouthed glass container or bowl. Add the strawberries and blood orange and stir to combine. Cover and set aside in cool, dark place until the vodka has taken on a fruity flavor and the strawberries have lost much of their color, 2 to 3 days.

2. Use tongs or a slotted spoon to remove as much of the fruit as you can. Line a funnel with a double layer of dampened cheesecloth; set over a pitcher or large bowl. Strain the infused vodka through; discard any solids. Pour the vodka into a clean bottle. Store at room temperature or refrigerate; it will keep indefinitely in the refrigerator.

SHRUBS: RUM OR COGNAC AND CHAMPAGNE

Recreated from eighteenth-century recipes by Walter Staib, owner of City Tavern, Philadelphia.

"But I do feel thirsty," said the poor lady, "and I do think a glass of shrub would do my throat good; it's dreadful dry. Mr. Peckham, would you be so polite as to pass me a glass of shrub?" Silas Peckham bowed with great alacrity, and took from the table a small glass containing a fluid reddish in hue and subacid in taste. This was shrub, a beverage in local repute, of questionable nature, but suspected of owing its tints and sharpness to some kind of syrup derived from a maroon colored fruit.

—Oliver Wendell Holmes, *The Event of the Season*

No half-measures are taken at City Tavern, an inn built in the 1770s that was reconstructed in 1994 for modern-day diners, while staying absolutely true to its historical foundations. Although the building is owned by the federal government and managed by the Department of the Interior and the National Parks Service, the restaurant is run by Concepts by Staib, Ltd., a company headed by Walter Staib.

Walter Staib took possession of City Tavern under the mandate that the reconstruction and renovation of the tavern had to be absolutely and completely as historically accurate as possible. Everything—the furnishings, decor, tableware, staff clothing, menu, food, and drink—had to conform to the years between 1774 and 1783. Walter did his homework thoroughly, researching every applicable topic germane to life during his historical window of interest, and hired culinary historian Dr. Lorna Sass to lend her expertise. "I kept seeing references to shrubs," says Walter, "but at first, I thought they were talking about bushes or foliage. When I realized that the shrub was a drink, I just had to try to re-create the drink for City Tavern."

Luckily for Walter, someone else had also done some homework on shrubs.

Tait Farm Foods, located in Centre Hall, Pennsylvania, is a grower, processor, and purveyor of uncommon specialty foods. From a small family farm, the Taits and their passionate helpers grow all of their crops using sustainable or organic methods and make unique food products in small batches, by hand. Their concentrated fruit shrubs, which Walter stumbled upon in a health-food store, are based on

authentic eighteenth- and nineteenth-century recipes and contain fruit vinegars (blueberry, cranberry, raspberry, strawberry, and apple) sweetened with sugar, honey, maple syrup, and spices. The result? Pure heaven. (For mail-order information, see page 131.)

With his eagle eye for historical integrity, Walter Staib offers shrubs at City Tavern made with rum, cognac, and champagne: all products available to the people, such as George Washington, John Adams, Thomas Jefferson, and Paul Revere, who visited this landmark inn during the eighteenth century. And these drinks, dating back further than the word *cocktail*, are among the most delightful, complex, intense potions in this book.

Shrubs may not be modern classics in the true sense of the term, but they are a sign of our times, when some stalwarts, people such as Walter and the good folk at Tait Farm Foods, are willing to go out of their way to preserve the past and offer a taste of our history to new generations of Americans.

RUM OR COGNAC SHRUB

makes 1 cocktail

1 ounce shrub

2 ounces dark rum or cognac

1 ounce club soda

Fill a stemmed goblet two-thirds full of ice cubes. Add the shrub, rum or cognac, and the club soda. Stir briefly, just to mix. Serve at once.

CHAMPAGNE SHRUB

makes 1 cocktail

2 ounces shrub

4 ounces chilled champagne

Pour the shrub and champagne into a flute. Stir only if the champagne fails to blend the ingredients thoroughly. Serve at once.

THE SINGLE-MALT SCOTCH MARTIN

makes 1 cocktail

3 ounces Oban single-malt scotch
$1/4$ ounce Tio Pepe fino sherry
1 lemon peel spiral, for garnish

Fill a mixing glass two-thirds full of ice cubes. Add the scotch
and sherry and stir until well blended and chilled. Strain into
a chilled cocktail glass; garnish with the lemon spiral.

THE SINGLE-MALT SCOTCH MARTINI

Created by Norman Bukofzer, head barman at the Ritz-Carlton Hotel, New York City, sometime in the late 1980s.

Walk into the bar at the Ritz-Carlton, New York, pull up a barstool, order whatever you fancy, and introduce yourself to head barman Norman Bukofzer. We guarantee that should you ever pass that way again Norman will know exactly who you are and what you drink. And if he really gets to know you, he will most likely find you an empty stool next to someone who will become a lifelong friend. Fortunately, Norman isn't the last of a dying breed, but he is one of the few examples of the old-time bartender—friendly, comically caustic at times, always ready with a quick comeback, capable of handling any situation at any given time—who also knows how to shake that shaker.

Norman says that he spent his first years as a bartender bumming around in resort hotels; but in 1982, he found his home at the Ritz-Carlton. These days, although the bar doesn't really have a name, regulars tend to know it as Norman's bar.

When the time comes for Norman to create, he tends to *feel* his way around. Ask him how he came up with any particular cocktail and usually he has no idea. His shoulders shrug, his eyes widen, and he says, "Just sort of sounded as though it would work." We have sampled many of Norman's creations, and usually he concocts some marvelous drinks, but none can match his Single-Malt Scotch Martini. Some think it's a sin to add anything other than a drop of spring water to a single-malt scotch; but Norman knows that if you use the best ingredients, you are sure to end up with a superior cocktail.

In the late 1980s, when single malts were becoming oh so popular, Norman wanted to find a way to serve single malts to customers who didn't want a snifter of neat whisky. Choosing Oban single malt, an incredibly flavorful spirit from the Western Highlands (it bears hints of peat and smoke and a magnificent waft of sea air), Norman turned to Tio Pepe, a dry fino sherry, and made a brilliant match. Of course, the connection between sherry and scotch is long formed—many malts, although not Oban, are aged in used sherry butts—but the fact that Norman chose Oban as the base liquor was nothing short of genius, and the soft scent of the lemon twist that Norman uses to garnish his creation adds that final touch of magnificence.

THE STARLIGHT

makes 1 cocktail

1 1/4 ounces Campari

1/4 ounce Cointreau

1/2 ounce freshly squeezed lemon juice

1/2 ounce freshly squeezed orange juice

1/4 ounce Simple Syrup (see page 10)

Club soda

1/2 ounce brandy

1 lemon wheel and 1 lime wheel, for garnish

1. Fill a large shaker two-thirds full of ice cubes. Add the Campari, Cointreau, lemon juice, orange juice, and simple syrup; shake until well blended and chilled.

2. Fill a 12-ounce collins glass half full of ice cubes. Strain the cocktail over the ice; add club soda to almost fill the glass. Float the brandy on top of the drink. Garnish with the lemon and lime wheels.

THE STARLIGHT

Created in 1996 by Tony Abou-Ganim, bartender at Harry Denton's Starlight Room, San Francisco (see also the Sunsplash, page 123).

Tony Abou-Ganim was seemingly destined to be a bartender when, in 1980, he found himself behind the bar at the Brass Rail, in Port Huron, Michigan. The restaurant had been opened by his aunt Helen David and her mother shortly after the repeal of Prohibition. "Customers at that time were still drinking Grasshoppers and Brandy Alexanders," recalls Tony. "And the Manhattans and Martinis that have recently made a comeback were very popular in those days, so my basic training was truly in the classics."

In 1985, with a business degree tucked firmly under his arm, Tony sought a career as a stockbroker in San Francisco. Tending bar helped pay the rent while he searched for the right job. "At one point I realized that bartending was going to be my career," he recalls. "And that's when I started to take the job seriously. Once I had made up my mind to be a professional bartender, I also started having more fun behind the bar. Strange how that works. In the bartending business, if you're not having fun, you aren't taking your job seriously enough.

The Starlight, named for Harry Denton's Starlight Room, is a crisp, refreshing cooler that gains much style and sophistication from the brandy that floats atop the drink. Don't sip this one through a straw—you'll miss the whole point of the drink.

THE STILETTO
makes 1 cocktail

1 1/2 ounces bourbon

1 1/2 ounces amaretto

1 ounce freshly squeezed lime juice

1 lime wedge, for garnish

Fill a shaker glass two-thirds full of ice cubes. Add the bourbon, amaretto, and lime juice; shake until well blended and chilled. Strain into a chilled cocktail glass or into an ice-filled old-fashioned glass. Garnish with the lime wedge.

THE STILETTO

Created by Al Romeo, beverage manager of Anthony's restaurant, Houston.

When Al Romeo talks about mixed drinks and cocktails, there are no pretensions in his voice, manner, or language; he just does what he does—mixology seems to be his favorite subject. Sure, talking is an important part of his job, but that's exactly what it is: *part* of his job. He's an old-timer for sure, and Al is a true professional.

After tending bar at Houston's Palm restaurant for fifteen years, Al joined the team at Anthony's in 1994, the year in which this Houston institution moved to a new location and was named by food, wine, and restaurant maven John Mariani as one of *Esquire* magazine's Best New Restaurants. Tony Vallone, owner of Anthony's, is probably the most renowned restaurateur in Houston; and Anthony's is reputed to be home to anyone who is anyone in that city's society circles. Tony was once rumored to have refused to serve Frank Sinatra, a report that gained him much publicity, but it just wasn't true. Apparently, Old Blue Eyes stayed in his car and sent his driver in for food simply because he was fresh off the golf course and didn't feel he was appropriately attired to join the crowd inside.

At first glance, the Stiletto is a simple drink, but take a closer look: There's something to it. Check the ingredients—bourbon, amaretto, and lime juice. When mixing a whiskey-based drink, lemon is most often the citrus juice of choice; but Al went with its greener cousin. Why? Now look at the proportions. There seems to be a lot of amaretto: Won't this drink be outrageously sweet? And there's the rub. The tart lime juice cuts right through the sweetness of the liqueur, leaving behind all of the almond flavors, which somehow execute a perfect turn with the bourbon. This is a tart, refreshing, adult drink. Its beauty lies in its simplicity.

Al Romeo stirs the Stiletto in an old-fashioned glass, but we prefer to shake it to thoroughly mix the juice with the liquors. We also recommend that you try the Stiletto straight up in a cocktail glass before dinner or on the rocks anytime—this drink is as refreshing a potion as you are likely to taste.

THE SUNSPLASH

Created in 1996 by Tony Abou-Ganim, bartender at Harry Denton's Starlight Room, San Francisco (see also the Starlight, page 119).

In San Francisco, Tony Abou-Ganim tended bar at the Balboa Café, the Blue Light, and Harry Denton's, until Denton was asked by hotel and restaurant entrepreneur Bill Kimpton to head up the operations at his newly reopened Starlight Room (now Harry Denton's Starlight Room) on top of the Sir Francis Drake Hotel. Tony, along with all the other bartenders at this sophisticated supper club, was brought up through the ranks of Harry Denton's before being offered a job at the Starlight Room.

"In 1996, when I was taking inventory, I noticed a surplus of Stolichnaya Ohranj," says Tony. "So I created the Sunsplash to tempt more of our customers to try this relatively new product."

The name came from two sources: the color and the fact that Tony's fellow bartender, Byron McWaters, owns a metalworks called Sunsplash. Tony says that it's sort of an insider name. "The Sunsplash is what I describe as a feel-good drink," says Tony. "And, although the ingredients may look whimsical, the resultant libation is both sophisticated and refreshing."

THE SUNSPLASH
makes 1 cocktail

2 1/2 ounces Stolichnaya Ohranj vodka

1/2 ounce Cointreau

1 ounce freshly squeezed lemon juice

1/2 ounce freshly squeezed orange juice

1/2 ounce cranberry juice

1/2 ounce Simple Syrup (see page 10)

1/2 orange slice and 1 lemon twist, for garnish

Fill a large shaker two-thirds full of ice cubes. Add the vodka, Cointreau, the juices, and the simple syrup; shake until well blended and chilled. Strain into an ice-filled goblet (or chilled cocktail glass); garnish with the orange slice and lemon twist.

THE TAPIKA COCKTAIL

makes 1 cocktail

1/2 ounce Cointreau
Coarse salt, for coating the rim of the glass
3 1/2 ounces Chinaco Blanco tequila
1/2 ounce prickly pear cactus syrup
(available at specialty food stores)
1 ounce freshly squeezed lime juice
1 thin lime wheel, for garnish

1. Pour the Cointreau into a cocktail glass. Use a bit of it to
moisten the outside of the rim of the glass. Swirl the liquor
around to coat the inside of the glass and then pour it out.
Lightly and evenly coat the moistened outside rim of the
glass with coarse salt.

2. Fill a large shaker two-thirds full of ice cubes. Add the
tequila, prickly pear syrup, and lime juice; shake until well
blended and chilled. Strain into the prepared glass. Float
the lime wheel on top.

THE TAPIKA COCKTAIL

Created in 1996 by executive chef David Walzog and
general manager Jason Lapin of Tapika, New York City
(see also the Chile Rita, page 35).

The Tapika Cocktail was created when
the long-awaited Chinaco tequila was finally made available in New York. Because they knew and loved the
flavor of this spirit, Jason and David decided to create
a drink in its honor. "Chinaco has a wonderful barbed
quality; and although we added just a touch of
Cointreau—a drier bottling than most triple secs—we
didn't want the drink to be too sweet," says Jason.
"Prickly pear juice was a natural choice to flavor this creation; it bears a certain sharpness that marries well with
the Chinaco."

David continues, "This is a wonderful drink for
springtime. We plan to create new drinks seasonally at
Tapika."

Legally, tequila can be made with as much as 49 percent sugar, although agave (a native Mexican plant
that is part of the amaryllis family and not, as many
believe, a type of cactus) must provide the predominant flavor. Chinaco, however, along with many other
bottlings of tequila that have been introduced in
recent years, is made from 100-percent agave. Look on
the label of any bottle of tequila: If it's 100-percent
agave, the words will be right there. We suggest that
you stick to the Chinaco Blanco bottling if you want to
savor the Tapika Cocktail as it is served at this wonderful restaurant; but feel free to experiment with other
100-percent agave bottlings if you so desire.

THE TART GIN COOLER
makes 1 cocktail

2 ounces London dry gin
2 ounces freshly squeezed pink grapefruit juice
3 ounces tonic water
2 dashes of Peychaud bitters

Fill a 12-ounce collins glass two-thirds full of ice cubes.
Pour in the gin, juice, tonic, and bitters; stir together
and serve at once.

THE TART GIN COOLER

Created serendipitously by us in 1996.

In Britain, soft drink companies sell what's called "bitter lemon," a carbonated beverage that's a combination of lemon flavoring and tonic water. Sometimes you can find it here, but it's easy enough to make for yourself. Simply add a touch of freshly squeezed lemon juice and a touch of simple syrup to tonic water. We sometimes sip on gin and bitter lemon during the summer months; but when working on a fruit drinks article for *Food & Wine* magazine, we started to blend all sorts of fruit juices with plain old tonic water.

The best match turned out to be our bitter pink grapefruit juice with a tot of London dry gin; but still, the drink needed an extra dimension, something to bring all the flavors together and add a little extra to the experience. Of course, in true bartender style, we turned to bitters. Bitters are to the bartender what salt and pepper are to the chef. Take our advice: If you concoct a cocktail that tastes good, but not superlative, add bitters. Try Angostura, Peychaud, or orange bitters; one of them will usually turn your creation into a drink fit for kings. Be sure to use London dry gin in this drink (the words are printed on the bottle), it is always more complex than compound gins since the botanicals—various herbs, fruits, and spices—are distilled into the gin. Compound gins are merely neutral spirits with added flavorings, usually flavored oils and the like.

In this particular case, Peychaud bitters turned out to be the ingredient that turned our Tart Gin Cooler into a complex, refreshing drink that we humbly deem worthy of being a new classic. This is a summertime drink: Sip it by the pool, gulp it on the deck, or mix it without the tonic water to take on a picnic. Simply top each drink off with tonic as you laze on the grass and watch the sun set.

THE UNI-SHOOTER

Created in 1988 by Daisuke Utagawa, owner of Sushi-Ko, "Washington, D.C.'s First Sushi Bar."

Daisuke Utagawa is a native of Tokyo who came to America as a youth, when his journalist father was here on assignment. After returning to Japan, where he attained certification as a sushi chef after training in some of Tokyo's top sushi restaurants, he returned to the United States, where he first worked as a sushi chef at Sushi-Ko and eventually bought the restaurant when the previous owner decided to retire. Sushi-Ko is one of the first restaurants in the United States. to carry a complete line of the boutique, hand-crafted sakes that are known as ji-sake. Ji-sake, traditionally served cold, not hot, is akin to micro- or craft-brewed beers as opposed to the mass-produced variety.

When you eat at Sushi-Ko, if you are feeling particularly daring, you may want to order a cup of Hire Sake. This traditional Japanese drink is made by adding two freshly grilled fugu (blowfish) fins—deadly if not prepared correctly—to a cup of almost boiling sake. The drink is ignited and immediately covered to extinguish the flame. When the flame dies it sucks all of the flavor from the blowfish fins; it's a great cold-weather drink, says Utagawa. Truthfully, you can order this drink at Sushi-Ko whether you feel daring or not; the fugu fins are expertly prepared by Daisuke's certified fugu chef, Kazuhiro "Kaz" Okochi.

The drink that you should always order at Sushi-Ko, providing you like sea urchin, is the Uni-Shooter. You won't find it on the menu; you have to have heard about it elsewhere. "I first made an Uni-Shooter after a discussion about oyster shooters with an old friend, Kim Glosserman," recalls Daisuke. "*Uni* is the Japanese word for 'sea urchin;' and I accidentally said 'uni' instead of 'oyster' during our conversation. We decided that, if there was no such thing as an Uni-Shooter, we should create one."

According to Daisuke, not everyone will enjoy the Uni-Shooter; but if you like sea urchin, this drink is for you. He recommends using Otokoyama ji-sake, chilled to white wine temperature, and says that this is a great drink to down during the course of a meal. It's sort of an intermezzo.

THE UNI-SHOOTER

makes 1 cocktail

2 ounces chilled premium sake

1 piece (about 1¹/₂ inches long) sushi-quality *uni* (sea urchin)

1 raw quail's egg yolk

1 small dab (about the size of a green pea) prepared wasabi

5 drops soy sauce

1 cucumber stick

1 piece (about 1 inch square) nori (seaweed), cut into fine slivers

1. Pour the sake into a chilled cocktail glass. Carefully add the *uni*; gently slide the egg yolk into the glass. Drop in the wasabi.

2. At the edge of the glass, release the drops of soy sauce so they form a brown cloud. Stand the cucumber stick in the glass. Just before serving, sprinkle on the slivered nori.

BIBLIOGRAPHY

Arthur, Stanley Clisby. *Famous New Orleans Drinks & how to mix 'em.* Gretna, LA: Pelican, 1989.

Bishop, George. *The Booze Reader: A Soggy Saga of Man in His Cups.* Los Angeles: Sherbourne, 1965.

Crockett, Albert Stevens. *The Old Waldorf-Astoria Bar Book.* New York: Crockett, 1935.

Embury, David A. *The Fine Art of Mixing Drinks.* 2nd ed. New York: Garden City Books, 1952.

Grimes, William. *Straight Up or On the Rocks— A Cultural History of American Drink.* New York: Simon & Schuster, 1993.

Mariani, John F. *The Dictionary of American Food and Drink.* New Haven, CT: Ticknor & Fields, 1983.

Mendelsohn, Oscar A. *The Dictionary of Drink and Drinking.* New York: Hawthorne Books, 1965.

Montagné, Prosper. *Larousse Gastronomique.* New York: Crown, 1961.

Sax, Richard. *Classic Home Desserts.* Shelburne, VT: Chapters, 1995.

Thomas, Jerry. *How to Mix Drinks or The Bon-Vivant's Companion.* New York: Dick & Fitzgerald, 1862.

Mail-Order Sources for Hard-to-Find Items

For orange bitters

Fee Brothers, Inc., 453 Portland Avenue, Rochester, NY 14605; Phone 800-961-FEES; Fax 716-544-9550.

For Peychaud bitters

Rebecca Green, The Sazerac Co., Inc., 803 Jefferson Highway, New Orleans, LA 70121; Phone 504-831-9450; Fax 504-831-2382.

For shrubs

City Tavern, 138 South Second Street, Philadelphia, PA 19106; Phone 215-413-1443.

Tait Farm Foods, RR 1, Box 329, Centre Hall, PA 16828; Phone 800-787-2716 or 814-466-2386.

INDEX